Spiritual Health Warning

2 Corinthians: Apostle's Prescription

Other books by Michael Baughen

Moses and the Venture of Faith
The Prayer Principle

SPIRITUAL HEALTH WARNING

2 Corinthians: Apostle's Prescription

MICHAEL BAUGHEN

MARSHALLS

Marshalls Paperback
Marshall Pickering Ltd.,
3 Beggarwood Lane, Basingstoke, Hants, RG23 7LP, UK

Copyright © 1982 by Michael Baughen

First published by Marshall Morgan & Scott in 1982
This edition issued in 1985

ISBN 0 551 01021 5

Printed and bound in Great Britain by
Hunt Barnard Printing Ltd, Aylesbury, Bucks

To my three families:

the human family I share with my wife Myrtle, and
   with Rachel, Philip and Andrew

the church family of All Souls, Langham Place,
   London in which I have shared as Rector and
   where 2 Corinthians burnt into my soul

the wider family of the Diocese of Chester in which
   I now share as Bishop

With thankfulness to God for all the love and
   encouragement experienced in all three families

and with particular thanks to Roger Barley, Helen
   Hartley and Pippa Dobson for their willing help
   in typing the manuscript for this book.

Contents

1: Introduction – the hot letter   9
2: Pressure and praise (1:2–2:13; 7:2–15)   14
3: Servants of the Lord (2:12–4:6)   26
4: Home or away (4:7–5:8)   42
5: Ambassador or passenger? (5:9–6:13)   57
6: Godly separation and godly sorrow
   (6:14–7:16)   73
7: 'Generous or stingy?' (Chapters 8 and 9)   83
8: War and captivity (10:1–11:13)   100
9: Power, grace and testing (11:16–13:14)   114

1: Introduction – The hot letter

This is the hottest letter of the New Testament! When you and I sit down to write a letter we usually face the prospect either with dragging feet or with eagerness. If it is a 'thank-you' letter for a birthday present we have to think what else to say, but if it is a love letter we can often go on and on – and on! – as our thoughts flow on to paper. Yet probably the most passionate of letters will be when we are deeply concerned for someone – perhaps they are in deep trouble, or are going astray in their lives, or are Christians who are compromising the faith. Then our writing will burn with the fire of loving concern. 2 Corinthians is that sort of letter. It is the most passionate and earnest of Paul's letters.

What is Paul so concerned about? The Corinthian church was active and apparently successful. There was plenty of love and zeal around, and lively worship with many people taking part. On the face of it, all was well. But Paul sees through the outer layer to what is going on underneath the surface and he is deeply concerned at what he discerns.

It may have been success that had gone to the Corinthians' heads. They were encouraged by a bunch of false teachers who had infiltrated the Corinthian church. Of course, they were not regarded as false by the Corinthians, but Paul could see the sort of people

9

they were. If you want to succeed as a false teacher in such a situation you first have to denigrate the previous teachers and instructors. In spite of all Paul had done for them the Corinthians were easily turned against him by these new teachers.

Their particular line was that if Paul was such a great apostle he ought to be living a triumphant trouble-free life. They argued, it seems, that Christians ought to be free of suffering, illness and the like – that the Christian life should be at a 'super' level. Now, they argued, Paul obviously was not up to that; he was consequently unworthy of the title of apostle and was not the sort of person to listen to or follow. These new teachers had something better to offer – a higher level of Christian living, a super-spirituality. The Corinthians liked this; it suited their pride. Paul counter-attacks in Chapters 1–4.

The false teachers had also lulled the Corinthians into an inactive faith. They had so encouraged a spiritual smugness, an inward-turned Christianity that was only concerned with its own joy, pleasure, excitement and satisfaction, that evangelism had taken a back seat. Paul is deeply concerned about this and powerfully argues for the 'today' of evangelism in this letter (Chapters 5–6). He must have known, as we know today, that any church which looks in on itself to the exclusion of outreach and concern for the world is a church that will die. Their attitude also made them careless towards the other churches and without concern for those parts of the church where there was urgent material need. Two whole chapters (8 and 9) of this letter are given over to the most powerful and persuasive argument for real Christian giving in the whole of the Bible.

Once you start emphasising feelings and experiences more than facts you have begun to walk a dangerous road. The Corinthians were proud of the special – even spectacular – spiritual experiences in their midst. Yet, as 1 Corinthians 15 tells us, they began to be less concerned about right doctrine. There were probably some who took the line that as long as you had the right sort of experience it did not matter too much what you believed. Perhaps they argued that Paul was too cerebral and they had found experience-centred Christianity to be much more satisfying. In 1 Corinthians 15 it is clear that they had grown careless about the truth of Christ's resurrection and like many today were saying that as long as you experienced the resurrection-life in yourself it did not matter very much whether Christ rose or not. Paul thunders against that in 1 Corinthians 15 and here in this second letter (especially chapters 10–13) he continues to express his deep concern that they should be clear on the fundamentals of the Christian gospel. Hand in hand with doctrinal truth is moral living that accords with the word of God. Their readiness to let moral error into their midst was alarming to Paul and has been an alarming feature of experience-centred Christianity ever since.

Churches that are cerebral and cold, without the warmth of real fellowship and sharing in the grace of Christ, are in need of spiritual fire. Churches that are experientially warm but have ceased to value expository preaching and in-depth teaching are in need of spiritual correction. This marvellous, urgent and ardent letter of Paul can awaken the first sort and correct the latter sort. It is a letter of outstanding relevance to the church of our day.

However, before we get into the richness of the letter we need to look at the opening greetings of the first two verses. These are not verses to 'skip' as unimportant. They teach us several important things. Firstly we must see the authority with which Paul writes. He designated himself as an apostle whereas

Timothy is called 'our brother' and the members of the church in Achaia are 'saints'. Although the title 'Apostle' was sometimes used in the more general sense as 'someone sent' it has primarily a very special significance in the New Testament, referring only to the Twelve and Paul. The apostles were all specially called by Christ – with Paul so called on the road to Damascus. They were marked out by God by the signs done through them (Acts 2:43) just as Jesus had been shown to be who he was by 'signs' (John 2:11). The church was 'built upon the foundation of the apostles and prophets, Christ Jesus himself being the cornerstone' (Ephesians 2:20). The successor to the apostles is the New Testament – this is where the apostolic doctrine is enshrined for ever and the 'apostolic succession' is the careful handing on of the apostolic truth.

The idea that we can have apostles today with similar authority to Paul is a grievous misunderstanding of the authority of the New Testament. The further teaching that such present-day apostles have equal authority in teaching to the New Testament apostles is heresy. What we handle here in 2 Corinthians is from the hand of one who was designated an apostle by Jesus Christ and so has the authority of God. We study it together, therefore, not as an interesting piece of writing but as the word of God to us – to hear and obey.

The letter is especially to the church at Corinth. 'Church' here is, of course, the local company of believers in the city of Corinth. They are not just a set of individuals but part of a group, a family, a body. Christianity is not an individual matter that we express sometimes with other individuals – it is baptism into the body of Christ and carries with it a mutual responsibility of love, care, encouragement and learning. Even the word 'saints' which Paul uses

of all the Christians in Achaia is a corporate word –
it is used sixty-three times in the New Testament,
always in the plural (except for one instance where it
is singular but the meaning is plural – Philippians
4:21). You cannot be an individual 'saint'. You are
part of God's people – those within his family – and
you are 'one of the saints' – one of those belonging to
the Lord. Your Christianity cannot therefore be on
your own in your own small corner – any more than
you can live in a human family and have nothing to
do with its other members. With Paul we must thus
be concerned not only with our own Christian lives
but also with the life and witness of the Church of
God – in our local area and worldwide. We are part
of it; we rejoice with it and weep over it; we pray for
it and work in it.

The grace and peace Paul wishes for his readers
extends to us. He wishes us to know that grace in all
its love, mercy, forgiveness, direction and kindness;
the overflowing grace into which we have been
brought and by which we are to grow and serve; and
the peace in the middle of every storm, every pressure
and every challenge . . . the peace which passes understanding and which comes from God alone.

2: Pressure and praise
1:2–2:13; 7:2–15

Paul does not waste a minute. He gets right into the burning theme of his heart: suffering. He will come back to it several times right through to the end of the letter. He knows more about suffering than all the false teachers put together. He knows it to be not a discredit to his apostleship but rather an evidence of his true following of Christ.

Jesus Christ was called 'the suffering servant' in Isaiah's prophecy. He did not tell his disciples that following him would be a blessed picnic in the sunshine, but that it means denying ourselves and taking up the cross. We are called to drink the cup of suffering as he did. The early disciples knew the most cruel persecution, suffering and ghastly deaths – torn to shreds by lions in the arena and even crucified. Suffering has been part and parcel of Christian testimony ever since and still is so today, across all the continents of the world.

Samuel Rutherford put it like this: 'God has called you to Christ's side and the wind is now in Christ's face in this land; and seeing you are with Him you cannot expect the lee-side or the sunny side of the brae.' Yet when you hear some evangelists and Christian testimonies you are led to expect only sunshine and milk and honey!

The key-word in this first chapter is 'troubles' (NIV) or 'affliction' (RSV) – the Greek word is *thlipsis* – in verses 4, 6, 8. It means 'pressure' – physical pressure from a heavy weight on our body, but also mental or spiritual pressure. It is certainly the word for modern man in today's world. We all seem to live under pressures. These are some of them: a) The pressure to 'conform' – Romans 12:1–2. The world wants us to conform, says Paul. The word he uses means 'pressure from without' like the pressure on the liquid jelly mixture to make it conform to the jelly mould. The world does not like 'non-conformists' and is irritated by the Christian who stands up for Christ's standards. It wants to squeeze us into its mould. The pressure from the media and from the opinion of our peers is enormous on us all.

b) The pressure of life itself – of illness, sorrows, bereavement, unemployment, starvation, poverty, disappointments, frustrations, wars, broken relationships, hopes and dreams unfulfilled. We share in this whether we are Christians or not, because we share in a fallen world.

c) The pressure of a world without Christ – the size of the evangelistic task, the wealth and power of the Arab States in promoting Islam, the spiritual blindness of our friends and relations, the untouched millions, the worship of materialism, the moral chaos. All this spells agony for the world.

d) The pressure of false teaching. Not only do we have to contend with atheism and apathy but with false teaching and heresy – the cults and similar movements that capture people in our city centres to make them prisoners of error.

e) The pressure of attacks upon us for our faith – of

persecution, being laughed at, mockery, sarcasm and being 'frozen out' by some of our friends.

See what a relevant word *thlipsis* is! You can no doubt add to the list within your own experience. As you do so, realize how much more Jesus felt this pressure. He saw sin with clarity and participated in a fallen world as one who had created the world in its unfallen state. How he must have felt the world's pressures – physical, mental and spiritual! In all this, but particularly when we suffer for our faith, 'the sufferings of Christ flow over into our lives'.

God's comfort

It would be natural to groan about suffering. It is never pleasant and all of us would like to be without it. The false teachers thought we ought to be without it and to be superior to such experiences; but the flaw in that sort of teaching is that it wants heaven now. We will only be truly free from pressure and suffering when we leave our bodies behind and go home to the Lord.

Others tell us we should praise God for suffering and that we can have the victory that way; but it is a way of deception and despair. So what does Paul do? He praises (verse 3) because he knows that whatever pressure comes on him and whatever sufferings he has to endure, the comfort of God outmatches it. That really is something to praise about! And it is Paul's genuine testimony – plus the testimony of millions since then.

What is comfort? The word is *paraklesis*. You will immediately recognize that as the same root as *par-aklete* – the description that Jesus gives of the Holy Spirit in John 13–16 ('Comforter' in the AV and 'Counsellor' in RSV). *Para* means 'alongside' and *'klesis'* means 'called'. So we can grasp from this what 'comfort' is all about. It is God coming alongside. It is not necessarily an altering of the pressure or trouble, though it may be that. What it always means is that special gracious presence of the Lord. The psalmist in Psalm 23 demonstrates this vividly. When he is by the still waters he says 'The Lord . . .' but when he passes through the valley of the shadow of death he says '*You* are with me.' The close personal relationship with the Lord intensifies in the experience of trial. Hasn't that been the testimony of Christians through the ages? 'The Lord was so close to me . . . I was marvellously supported by the Lord . . . I have come to know the Lord more closely and intimately through this experience.' And is this not why, when we think of the most wonderful Christians we have met, we usually think of those who have gone through suffering and have glowed with the faith and love of Jesus? As Psalm 84 put it: 'As they pass through the valley of Baca (suffering) they make it a place of springs – the autumn rains also cover it with pools.' I was fascinated as I flew across the desert between the Grand Canyon and Las Vegas in the USA to see pools of water dotted around in this otherwise parched area. This psalm came to mind – so did the Christians I have known who have gone through a desert experience in life and have drunk deeply of the wells of God's comfort and grace.

Certainly there is no stinginess about the comfort God gives – as he comes alongside – and it is the lovely testimony of Paul (verse 5) that 'as the sufferings of Christ flow over into our lives, so also through Christ our comfort overflows.' 'Overflows' – not just a small quantity, nor even carefully measured out but full and running over!

Comfort is for sharing

There is all the difference between a Euston experience and a Crewe experience. If you are a British railway enthusiast like me you will know exactly what I mean, but for others I will need to explain. These drawings may help:

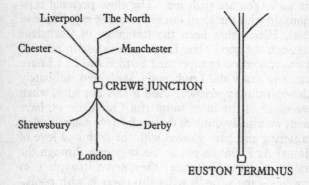

Euston is a terminus. All trains stop there and can go no further. It is the end of the line and the final destination of all trains.

Crewe is a junction. Some trains terminate there but most of them go on. You can change at Crewe. Going north the lines branch off to Liverpool, or to Preston and Scotland, or to Manchester, or to Chester and North Wales. Going south you can branch to Shrewsbury, or to Derby or to London.

Paul says here, in effect, that comfort is to be a Crewe and not a Euston. It is (verse 4) 'so that we can comfort those in any trouble' or (verse 6) 'if we are distressed it is for your comfort and salvation; if we are comforted, it is for your comfort'.

It is important to get hold of this. It is natural to want comfort in Euston terms. We want comfort for ourselves. We are going through this experience and we are the terminus and destination of all the comfort God likes to bring. But Paul pushes us to see that although part of the destination is us, we are also to be comfort junctions, sharing and passing on to others the comfort that came to us.

It seems likely that Christians may experience more suffering than non-Christians, rather than less suffering, because of the value it brings in comfort ministry. It is not easy to share comfort with others if you have not had illness or suffering. As the old Arab proverb puts it: 'All sunshine makes a desert.'

Learning to comfort

Of course, it helps if the affliction someone else is experiencing is identical with what we have been through – if we can say 'We had miscarriages too' or 'We know what mental illness is like too' or 'We know what it means to lose a child relative in an accident.' But we are not confined to what we have suffered. The principles and experience of comfort are to help us comfort others 'in any trouble' and we are to bring to bear 'the comfort we ourselves have received from God' (verse 4). This puts upon us the responsibility of learning through God's comfort and observing what has really helped us.

We may be devastated by the death of a husband or wife – and the aching void goes on and on. At the same time, as we draw on God's comfort, we should take note so that we can help others going through the same valley later. Sometimes God's comfort is very practical, like the cake and water for the spiritually depressed Elijah, rather than a sermon or a text. Sometimes it is the quiet presence of a friend in Christ that means more to us than talking. Learn from the way God comforts you – directly and through others – and so become a more effective minister of comfort to others for Christ.

Troubles can increase your faith

In verses 8–11 we see Paul getting even more blessing out of affliction. The experience itself was as bad as it could be. He described it vividly as being so unbearable that they believed they were going to die. J. B. Phillips translated it: 'We told ourselves that this was the end.' The word he uses is that used to describe a ship sinking under a load or of people breaking under strain. We might describe it as 'the bottom dropping out of my life'.

Some years ago I was a leader at a boys' camp in Surrey. They were lively youngsters aged ten to thirteen. We went down to Littlehampton for the day and there by the sea was a large amusement park with dodgems, a big dipper and much more. Up came one of the boys. 'Come on the rotor, sir?' I did not know what the rotor was, but I could not think of a way of saying 'No' to the boy and not looking a coward! So I yielded. 'Here, sir,' he said, and led me through a door into a very large drum. People were looking over the top with disconcerting grins on their faces! 'Just stand against the wall, sir.' I did. 'It'll go round in a minute, sir.' It did. And as it speeded up and I was spreadeagled against the wall, wishing I had never said 'Yes', he added with an impish grin, 'They'll take the floor away in a minute, sir!' They did! I remained pinned to the wall by the force of the rotor. That was (almost!) Paul's experience here. The floor had dropped away – he despaired of life itself.

So what happened? Did he argue with God? Did he complain or moan at God? Did he say, 'Why has this happened to me?' No! Instead, with the certain touch of someone close to God, he sees that such an experience had a purpose (v. 9): 'that we might not rely on ourselves but on God, who raises the dead'. In the tidal wave of troubles when many Christians would give up, Paul, like many since, threw himself upon God. No one else could deliver him. Rather than losing faith in such a moment, he had faith to the uttermost.

Help! Start praying!

Paul looks back upon that time in Asia and is thankful that God delivered him. And he goes on learning and applying. Now he is going through a similar experience, he does not start from square one. He begins with what he learnt last time. He sets his hope (verse 10) on deliverance this time too and he encourages the Corinthians to help and share with their prayer (they were more inclined to criticise). Paul can see even further blessing resulting – because if many people pray then many people will share in the praise and thanksgiving when God answers.

That is a lesson for us to learn in our churches. The prayer gathering should be the humming powerhouse of the church. There we are to share the challenges and the needs in real prayer and there we shall go on giving thanks and praise as God answers prayer in different ways. Some of the most joyful and tearful (tears of joy) times I have shared with fellow Christians have been after God has brought us together through a great venture of faith or has met with someone in the congregation in a special way. I was visiting a church recently where on the previous Sunday the church family had wept in prayer for a child member who had been knocked down in an accident and was on the verge of death; but God had wonderfully met with the child and them all and on this Sunday they were overwhelmed with praise and thanksgiving.

Sometimes we have to be brought to the point of helplessness to realize how our faith is shot through with dependence on our skills, our talents or the support of the fellowship. I tussled with a man for weeks as he looked at the Christian faith. He was then afraid to come to Christ because of the cost to himself and his businesses. He could see that Christ was Saviour and Lord; but could also see it would mean his becoming honest and that this would result in financial ruin. After getting in his car and driving 'anywhere' in the night to get away, he came back and yielded to Christ in my rectory at midnight. The honesty that resulted almost ruined him – almost. It came to the point of the bailiffs arriving on his doorstep to evict his family and take possession of his goods. God stepped in. He and his wife rebuilt their lives with Christ, and the lesson they learnt in that overwhelming affliction has been well applied ever since in their committed lives. They have learnt and relearnt that such experiences of overwhelming affliction are 'to make us rely not on ourselves, but on God who raises the dead'.

Who'd be a leader? (1:12–2:11, and 7:2–15)

It is always so sad when affliction comes to us from fellow Christians. When we are in positions of Christian leadership we are often the recipients of unloving action, bitter criticism, hurtful misrepresentation and wounding misunderstanding. I sometimes wonder whether some people feel they can fire their guns at Christian leaders because they do not think he or she should fire back!

Paul does not fire back but he does not let them go on in their misunderstanding either – he takes time to explain and plead from the heart. As he says in chapter 2 verse 5, pain of this kind affects everybody.

It is not just the person attacking or being attacked; others are caught up in the battle and the pain of one member affects the whole body. Healing therefore has to come to the whole body and Paul sets out to achieve this. So what may we learn?

a) *You must love – even if you fail in everything else* (1:15–2:1). The Corinthians had accused Paul of vacillation. He had said he would come to them on his way to Macedonia and he had not done so. Could his 'yes' and 'no' be trusted? That really is unfair, says Paul. His 'yes' and 'no' were utterly reliable. He was someone who stood on the promises of God, was commissioned to serve God and was, like the Corinthians, sealed by the Holy Spirit. He did not say one thing and mean another. They had misconstrued the events. Paul had indeed changed his plans but not deceitfully or carelessly – he had done so out of sheer love for them. He had felt that a visit from him would have caused them more pain and he wanted to spare them that pain. Instead of coming to them he had decided to write a letter to them and this was difficult enough for him. He wrote (2:4) out of 'great distress' (it is *thlipsis* again) and anguish of heart and with many tears. His love for them was overflowing.

Soon after I was first ordained I had to go to a home to explain the disciplinary action we were having to take against a teenage son of that family. Afterwards the mother said 'If only he had said it with love.' It was a fair rebuke. It is so much easier to discipline without love. We must not do so. Down through the years of my ministry since then I have had to act with discipline in several complex situations. I have normally been able to share that action with my church-wardens or other close counsellors or fellow ministers. It has always been immensely costly to act; the pain has often kept me awake as I have wondered what to

23

do and how to do it. The hurt to the body of the church family – when the situation has been known – has been deep. Yet the deepest concern is that we might act with a right balance of discipline and love.

b. *Love has to be shown by the body to the defaulter.* There comes the point (2:6–11) when restoration must begin. This is not possible without genuine sorrow and penitence, but clearly the person concerned here (v. 7) has shown deep sorrow for his act. Back in 1 Corinthians 5:5 the man had been 'delivered to Satan for the destruction of the flesh that his spirit may be saved'. Now, he ought to be drawn back into the fellowship with true forgiveness or else Satan will get into the church – presumably by bringing a spirit of hardness and lack of love. Paul is alert to the devices of Satan and elsewhere (Ephesians 4:26–27) he warns that letting the sun go down on our wrath gives opportunity to the devil. How closely we need to keep to the heart and mind of Christ in such complex and sensitive situations in the church. In the end, the painful incident was only cleared up by action, love and involvement. To have ducked the issue and not acted would have left a festering sore to poison the whole body. Action had to be taken – but in deepest love.

c) *The Christian leader feels the most pain.* When we are ultimately responsible – humanly – then we feel things the most deeply. There is no other human being to whom we can pass the buck. We may get advice and share with others; we will pray and wait on the Lord; but in the end we have to carry the matter on our heart. Paul does that. So in verses 12 and 13 of chapter 2 he tells us that even though he had an open door for the gospel he could not rest. He was longing to know what had happened and how the church had reacted. No telephones or telegrams to speed the news! So he went off to Macedonia to see if he could meet up with Titus who had been sent to Corinth.

We have to turn on to chapter 7:2–16 to see the sequel. There we learn that even in Macedonia he had no rest – but 'conflicts on the outside; fears within' (recognise the 'fightings without and fears within' from the hymn 'Just as I am'?) until Titus came. Then such joy and comfort! The Corinthians had shown a godly grief and had been earnestly ready to get things straight. Titus had been overjoyed about their reaction and his mind was set at rest by it all. So Paul is full of joy, comfort and peace – his heart goes out to them: 'You have such a place in our hearts that we would live or die with you.' Perhaps their hearts could be more open towards Paul, but still Paul is overjoyed. Once again, but in different circumstances, he can testify (7:4) that with all the trouble he is filled with comfort – his 'joy knows no bounds'. No wonder he could begin (chapter 1 verse 3) with the testimony from the depths of his heart: 'Praise be to the God and Father of our Lord Jesus Christ, the Father of compassion and the God of all comfort, who comforts us in all our troubles, so that we can comfort those in any trouble, with the comfort we ourselves have received from God.'

3: Servants of the Lord
2:12–4:6

There is no greater privilege for any human being than to serve the Lord – though from the way some Christians act, you would think it was a nuisance! Never lose your sense of awe and wonder at the fact that God, your God, the God of the universe and eternity, is relying on you. So when we are helping others in his name, or speaking, or helping in a camp, or using our talents, we should see it as a holy privilege. This whole letter throbs with the heart of a man on fire with love for Christ and totally committed to use his life in the Lord's service. He does not kick around in the shallows but strikes out into the deep; he does not offer God his leftovers of time and energy but gives the best.

Paul is also deeply conscious that he does not serve alone. He is a worker with God, co-operating with the Holy Spirit and ministering a gospel that is brought alive in people's hearts and lives by the Spirit. He is deeply aware of his responsibility to handle God's truth faithfully and not casually. He knows that the Holy Spirit will not honour the mishandling of the truth.

Where should we serve him?

'Guidance' is a theme of interest to every Christian. Advertise a talk on guidance and people will pack in to listen. There is always rapt attention. Several times a week I talk to individuals about their life and God's guidance. Here is a young man in his first job. He is ill at ease and feels he is in the wrong job. Here is someone sensing a call to service on the world mission field – is it of God or not? Here is someone seeking advice about a personal relationship. The questions abound. The important factor is that such questions are being asked – that people really do want to know God's will for their lives. If you are not asking such questions then there is something wrong with your commitment.

There is no straight rule-of-thumb on guidance. It is a matter of balancing inward conviction with outward circumstances – surrounding everything with heartfelt prayer and a real submission to God. Here in 2:12–13 is one glimpse of guidance. Paul finds an open door to preach the gospel in Troas but does not stay because he has no inward peace. Thus when we find an open door for ministry it may not always be right to step through it. There are open doors in countless directions. The need and opportunity to preach or serve in one town is matched by the need in ten thousand other towns. Paul said goodbye to the people in Troas and set off for Macedonia. If he had been at peace in his heart then presumably he would have stayed put in Troas to take up the opportunity there. He would have continued until either the circumstances changed or the inward peace departed from him.

Christians should not flit about like butterflies merely to enjoy different spheres of action for Christ. Sometimes God calls us to stay in the same place and in the same task for him throughout our entire lives. To move would be to step outside the will of God. However, here in 2:12 Paul did not have the matching up of outward circumstances and inward peace. His lack of peace was due to the great concern he had about the Corinthians and all the pain in his heart about them. He had no way of finding out what was happening. Titus was not there at Troas and Titus was the person who could tell Paul the situation. The absence of Titus at that moment was itself a segment in the pattern of guidance. Until the Corinthian situation is sorted out Paul could not be at peace. It is not a simple 'casting all our care on the Lord' that will sort this kind of situation out. It needs healing action. Fellowship had been ruptured. Until it was repaired there could be no real peace in service. In a similar way Jesus tells us in his Sermon on the Mount (Matthew 5:23) that if we are offering a gift at the altar and there remember that our brother has something against us, that we should first go and be reconciled to our brother before offering the gift.

Remember you are on the King's side! (2:14)

In spite of having to leave Troas and its 'open door' Paul did not trail around with a look of failure on his face. He was 'always' in Christ's triumphal procession. So whether he was on the boat across to Macedonia, or was waiting at the quayside, or was spending the night at a hostelry (the predecessor of the motel!) he was still Christ's man. His Christian life was for always, not for sometimes.

We all find it a temptation to live in compartments, with the Christian side dominant at suitable times but neatly packed away when it is inconvenient. There are many who entirely separate their 'business life' from their 'Christian life'. It is an impossible separation in God's eyes. We are his servants *always* and should be bringing our Christian faith to bear in every section of our lives. In 1975–6 when we rebuilt All Souls, Langham Place in London the architect was a fine Christian as well as a brilliant architect. He insisted that at every site meeting we began in prayer. The tough builders, engineers and subcontractors soon got used to it and as time went on began to see that God was significantly answering prayer in the detail of what was happening on the building. They knew that the church members were praying with expectancy and determination. The brief prayer at those site meetings made them see this as more than a job and that was their own testimony about it at the end. This was all because the architect was unafraid to bring his living Christian faith into the business arena. Let 'always' be written across our own lives!

The King has triumphed

We are part of a 'triumphal procession' (2:14). We need some background to make this picture live for us. Such processions were frequent in the world of Paul's day. The Romans loved such events and did them in style. The really great processions were reserved for the returning conquerors and none was so magnificent as in Rome itself. Let your imagination capture the scene. The long straight road is lined with crowds of people in a mood for celebration. The talk is about the great victories won by the army and about the skill of the commander of that army. It is the commander who is honoured over all and rides on his chariot at the centre of the procession. His immediate family may ride with him or near him. There are two other groups of people in the procession. The army is there, marching upright and proudly, enjoying the celebration of their commander's victory. But the conquered are there too. They are shown off to the crowd – walking with drooping shoulders – defeated and captive – heading for death or slavery.

Paul puts Christ at the centre of this picture. What greater victor is there than Christ? What greater triumph is there to celebrate than his? At the name of Jesus every knee will bow and everyone will acknowledge him to be the Lord – whichever part of the procession they find themselves in. As the victory was won upon the cross, the triumphal procession has already begun. Paul sees himself (and we must see ourselves) as part of it so that wherever he goes and whatever he does for Christ in this world is in the context of that victory procession. Even his diversion from Troas to Macedonia is still in that triumph procession for we are 'always' in it, wherever we go. Every Christian is part of the family of Christ – and so we all walk in the joy of his triumph.

But there are others in that procession and Colossians 2:15 describes them: 'Having disarmed the powers and authorities, he made a public spectacle of them, triumphing over them by the cross.' So when we rejoice in the triumph of Christ – and we must always so rejoice – we declare the conquest of Satan and the legions of evil, and we declare that there is a greater power than theirs. The King has triumphed – for ever!

You have an aroma!

The advertisers make sure we are conscious of 'body odour' or of 'bad breath' and they are keen to persuade us to use perfume and after-shave, each with a special aroma or fragrance. We are not unaccustomed to the spreading of fragrance.

Paul's picture in 2:14 is not of after-shave of course! It is the smell of the incense that filled the air as it was disseminated by the priests. Yet Paul applies the picture personally. Those who are 'in Christ' are involved in spreading the fragrance of the knowledge of Christ. Just as people become conscious of a woman wearing perfume or of a man with strong after-shave, so others are to become conscious of the fragrance of Christ when they meet us. We are to have about us that 'unmistakable something' – the aroma of Christ. It is the fragrance of his love. In 1 Corinthians 13 we are reminded that great speaking or martyrdom is useless without love. The Christian who is to serve the Lord must have a life that breathes Christ or else his words are empty.

The essence of this fragrance is 'the knowledge of Christ'. That is not a dissemination of information but a demonstration of the personal fellowship with Christ in our lives. For many people there is a big jump from an 'arm's-length' knowledge of Christ to a personal knowledge of him. A few years ago I was at a conference of ministers and lay-readers. It was a big conference and had observers and reporters present from different church traditions. At the end of the conference a lady reporter from a church newspaper said, at the meal-table, 'What I cannot get away from is the fact that everyone here seems to know Christ personally.' That was a lovely testimony to the fragrance of the knowledge of Christ spread through many lives. It is vital that we spread such fragrance. Even though many may disagree with what we say, oppose what we say, and even mock what we say, they cannot deny the genuineness of a Christ-centred life.

Recently I have had a spate of letters from a mother about her daughter. The daughter has come to Christ and has become a lovely Christian, caring, serving and radiating Christ. Because of incidents earlier in life when the parents caused harm to the daughter, the mother cannot accept that her daughter does not condemn them. She is angry that the daughter is so loving and kind! I thank God that this girl's life spreads the fragrance of the knowledge of Christ.

The aroma has contrasting effects

Some of those perfume advertisements on TV are highly entertaining – like the man so affected by the girl's perfume that he leaps like Tarzan across the room with disastrous effects on a plate-glass window! The incense in the Roman General's procession had contrasting meanings. To the soldiers and the conqueror's family it signified victory. To the captives it signified defeat and death. The results are similar in Christ. The aroma of Christ spread by Christians reaches two sorts of people (2:15): 'Those who are being saved and those who are perishing'. The effects are that the first smell the aroma as a fragrance of life; the others as a fragrance of death.

It is the fragrance of life that draws Christians together wherever they meet. There is no other fellowship like this in the world. You can be in almost any part of the world and find fellow-believers and an immediate oneness in Christ that minimises other differences of language, colour or culture. You meet someone in a coach or a plane and find they are also a Christian. There is an immediate rapport. We are part of a worldwide fellowship of those who are, like us, 'in Christ'. We are drawn together by that very fragrance.

Yet at the same time, the person rejecting Christ finds the aroma of Christ an irritant. He does not like it. He resents it and is often angered by it. This is because it acts as a convicting fragrance. Deep down he has tried to bury any faith he might have had, and you remind him of it by your life. Hence, the persecution or antagonism can often be sharpest from those who once had some spiritual awareness and now have rejected Christ. We should be ready for this but should also welcome it as it is a sign of the convicting work of the Spirit going on in that person's life. There is hope!

A student comes to living faith at university and then goes home in the vacation to godless parents. Their reaction is predictably one of horror and antagonism. They do not rejoice in the transformed life, the improved morals and the new values – they only react. They are being convicted by the fragrance of Christ in the life of their son or daughter.

The Lord smells the aroma

Back in the Old Testament we have the picture of Noah's sacrifice after the flood and of this being a 'sweet-smelling savour' to God. There is a feel of the same idea here in verse 15 where it speaks of our being 'to God' the aroma of Christ. It is a lovely thought that our spreading the fragrance of Christ by our lives brings delight to the Father. He loves to see Jesus being uplifted and honoured. We bring joy to him when our lives are effectively encouraging other believers or convicting unbelievers. This influencing of others is possible for every Christian. It is not just the task of the preacher or the evangelist or the leader. They are included, of course, but so are you. Wherever you live and whatever you do – whether you are in a quiet secluded sphere or you are in a position of authority – you are to spread the fragrance of Christ by the way you live. And the Father will be delighted.

33

Who is equal to such a task?

Paul asks this question in verse 16. It is a right question to ask. I was taking a group of students, all preparing for ordination, to a tough city area in the north of England. They were to spend a day visiting house to house in that area. As the coach passed through the outskirts of the city, the tension grew. Suddenly, a student at the front of the coach, hands rustling rapidly through the pages of his New Testament, called out, 'Where is that text: "Who is equal to such a task?"?' We all had empathy with his cry! Which of us can possibly be equal to any task for Christ – but particularly in the context of this verse, the task of spreading the fragrance of Christ by our lives. How can I do it – in the office, the hospital, the university, the shop, the home and neighbourhood? You and I cannot do it on our own. The answer to the question is given by Paul in chapter 3 verse 5: in the NIV, 'our competence comes from God' but in the RSV, 'our sufficiency comes from God'. That is it. I am cast back day by day upon the Lord. In my own strength I cannot be equal to this task of spreading the aroma of Christ. It is only possible if I am daily refilled by his Holy Spirit and as the Holy Spirit transforms me gradually towards the measure of the stature of the fullness of Christ.

Spread the word

If people are awakened to the knowledge of Christ in our lives it is vital that we match that by a faithful sharing of the word of God and by showing others the light of the gospel. It is a partnership task between the ministry of the word and the ministry of the Holy Spirit. However accurate we may be in preaching the word it is useless unless the Spirit brings light.

We may spend a long time explaining the gospel to a friend or contact and then at the end they say, 'Yes, I must try harder!' We feel we have failed. Yet, the reason may be that our work has not been matched by the work of the Spirit. We need to surround each such conversation with prayer, training ourselves to use one half of the mind to speak and converse, the other half to pray.

Don't be a peddler (2:17)

There is now a strong warning about how *not* to handle the word of God. The peddler was a hawker, a street salesman, and often a cheat. Most of us will have seen such peddlers in action. We admire their skill and wit. They can persuade you that junk is valuable and seem to be able to sell the 'rubbish', simply by their selling techniques and clever tongue. One mark of such peddlers, according to Plato, is that they praise all their stock whether it is good or bad for the purchaser.

The church has always been plagued with peddlers of the word. They are very similar to the market peddler. They are supremely confident that their brand of Christianity or their divergent emphasis or their special super-spirituality is the only way. It is painful to see heresies operating like this. Like the peddler, these 'super-spiritual' people lose discernment. Anything labelled with their brand of thinking is regarded as acceptable and anything not so branded is unacceptable. They like quick results. The peddler wants an immediate purchase before he moves on.

The Christian 'peddler' is often concerned with 'scalps' – pressurising people into decisions and then leaving others to sort out the damage later. It is devastating to see the work of patient sowing and nurturing destroyed in an evening by forced evangelism or by false 'healing' or 'deliverance'. The peddler is often dishonest with his manipulation of his goods; he uses sleight of hand and a slippery tongue. That is readily done by the Christian 'peddler'. He manipulates the word and is often an attractive speaker or writer. People believe he must be right because 'he puts it over so well'. The false apostles plaguing the Corinthian church were such peddlers and the destruction had been painful.

It is easy to attack such peddlers of the word, but let us look to ourselves. Do *we* peddle the word? Are *we* guilty of manipulation or selectivity that does not take account of the whole truth of God? Paul reaffirms his stand in chapter 4 verse 2, 'We have renounced secret and shameful ways; we do not use deception, nor do we distort the word of God.'

Speak with God's authority (2:17)

'We speak before God with sincerity, like men sent from God.' This usually dawns on us slowly. We may begin by sharing the word of God with others, perhaps in a small study group. We may even proclaim the word and speak in meetings. We are conscious of our friends, our minister, our non-Christian hearers. Only slowly do we begin to be conscious of God and our responsibility to him, realizing that we are handling his word and in his sight. For me this has made preaching an ever-increasing privilege and an ever-increasing burden – a burden of the responsibility of handling God's word to others.

There is a special sense in which Paul could describe himself as called by God to this task, as an apostle. There is a special call, too, for ministers in the church. Yet the task is for the whole church. The force of the verse is that when we do it we should not do it apologetically, nor weakly, but 'like men sent from God'.

Authority geared to a manipulation of the word is dangerous but authority geared to a sincere submission to the word is dynamic. I use 'submission' deliberately. It is easy to impose our ideas on to the word and to think it is saying what we want it to say. It is another thing to submit to the word, to work at it and to dig and chew until we thoroughly grasp what God is saying. Then, when we share that we can do so with his authority.

When I was first ordained I found myself cornered by the opinions of people more than by the word of God itself. There was an accepted pattern and interpretation and if you stepped outside that you were written off as 'liberal'. Then I was invited to join a group of ministers under the age of forty who met to discuss together. Submission to scripture was the only rule. My first meeting was liberating! Here accepted ideas were discussed and often challenged, from the basis of what the Bible taught. One notable minister, a leader in the church, made a statement at one point and then, to my amazement, a much younger minister challenged him. The older man looked at the Bible passage being quoted by the younger man and then humbly said: 'You are right, my brother.' I was amazed – and thrilled. Here at last were those who had a sincerity about the word of God. It was a release to my whole ministry and to my spiritual life.

God's letter writing

Our job is to be postmen for Christ. A letter from Christ is to be delivered (3:3). It is a letter written by the Holy Spirit and it is written on to human hearts. We cannot do the writing, but we are involved in the delivery. We speak the word: the gospel of Jesus, his free offer to every human being. The Spirit makes it alive in the hearer.

How wonderful! It is always a marvel to me when I see this happening in a person's life. There are special times when we have opened the word of God to someone and they see and believe. The greatest miracle we can ever know is the miracle of spiritual rebirth. Often when I have 'been there at the birth' I am still astounded at the wonder of what God is doing in that person's life, in response to faith. Then a day or two later I see them and it is so clear in their life that the Holy Spirit really has brought them into Christ. The letter from Christ has truly been written on their heart. They are their own testimony to what has taken place.

The Corinthians wanted 'letters of recommendation' (3:1–3). Paul says: Look! see all these converts and their growth in the Spirit – they are sufficient recommendation. It amazes me that even in this very day there are those who write various churches off because they do not have this or that mark or have not 'spiritually arrived' in some people's eyes, and yet God is doing a tremendous work in the lives of many many people in those churches. That is God's recommendation and it is the only one that matters!

This passage teaches us the limits of our task. We are not commissioned to speak with our own competence but with the competence of God and his new covenant. We are not to water down, adapt or replace this word of God. The methods of delivery may alter but not what we deliver.

What happens in the believer's heart, by the Spirit, is for ever. That moment of faith and rebirth is entry into eternal life. It is not going to fade tomorrow morning. Chapter 3 verses 7–11 compares the glory of the old covenant through Moses with this new covenant through Christ. This new one will never fade – it lasts for ever. Let this thrill your soul! That night when you helped someone into real faith in Jesus was the beginning of that new life for ever in them – a moment therefore of colossal significance and results!

Target for change

The Spirit not only brings us to life for ever but he begins a work of transformation now. Verses 17–18 speak of the freedom he brings. The world thinks that becoming a Christian is entering into law-keeping but the Spirit shows that it is the beginning of true freedom – freedom from the world's conformity and into a new relationship with the Lord.

The partnership between the word and the Spirit now continues. On our side we are to 'contemplate' (NIV margin) the Lord's glory. The word means 'gazing into' like a mirror and thus can be translated 'reflect' as in the main text of NIV. The force is the same. The more we contemplate the Lord's glory – that is, who he is, what he did for us on the cross, and all he has shown us of himself in his word – the more we shall find the Spirit transforming us. The transforming is not automatic without our co-operative contemplating. Gradually over the years, as we know more of him through sermons, Bible exposition, study, meditation, so the Spirit changes us towards the likeness of Christ. To be like Christ – that is the target of every believer. The Spirit takes us towards that target.

This is the most important and wonderful thing that can happen to a human being and this is the gospel we offer. It is not barren theory but spiritual reality. It is evidenced in hundreds of thousands of lives. It is for real. So (4:1) 'we do not lose heart'. How could we? Instead we are the more strongly urged to ensure that our task of delivering the letter is done as Christ intends. Paul renews his commitment, and we must renew ours at the same time (4:2–3), to renounce any deception or distortion in ministering the word of God and to ensure that by 'setting forth the truth plainly' we 'commend ourselves to every man's conscience in the sight of God'.

Barriers to overcome

Paul reminds us now of the opposition. We might otherwise get carried away with euphoric expectation that all we had to do was to preach the word faithfully and then the Spirit would bring every hearer to life. We know that it is not so simple as that and Paul tells us why in 4:3–4. He has already spoken of it in connection with the Israelites in 3:13–16. We have an enemy! He is (v. 4) 'the god of this age'. He brings a blindness to the minds of unbelievers. Though the light of the gospel shines in the lives of believers and in their sharing of the gospel message, the result can be negative. Eyes may see but minds are blinded. Other philosophies guard the mind's door, prejudice jams it shut, sin nails it to its portals, darkness blocks out the light.

We must be clear about this barrier. Otherwise we might blame the gospel. There are many who have adapted the gospel to suit modern man. But that is hopeless. It is not the gospel that needs changing. I was travelling through Austria and came suddenly to a road tunnel. It was a bright sunny day outside but once in the tunnel I could not see. I panicked for a moment. I blamed the Austrian roadbuilders. Then I remembered I had my sunglasses on. There was nothing wrong with the tunnel – only with my ability to see. So it is with the gospel. The barriers that have to be removed are not in the gospel but in man. This is a spiritual warfare and the battle is only won by spiritual weapons – by prayer.

Calvin put it like this: 'The blindness of unbelievers in no way detracts from the clearness of his gospel, for the sun is no less resplendent because the blind do not perceive its light.'

Let there be light

The veil on the face (3:16) is only taken away when a person turns to the Lord. That veil rests on everybody outside Christ.

This, then, is a further incentive to get on with the task of preaching Christ. There is no more urgent task. Only through faith in him can the veil be removed and the blindness be taken away. Although we are reminded that not every preaching of Christ will bring results yet we are also reminded that it *is* the only way results can come. There is no other way. So we are encouraged to get on with preaching 'not ourselves' but 'Jesus Christ as Lord' (4:5). We are further encouraged in chapter 4 verse 6 by the reminder that the God we are serving is the same God who brought light into the world in the mighty act of creation. So reaching into the hearts of unbelievers is a small thing by comparison! We are also reminded that he shone into *our* hearts and has opened us up to know him.

With such incentives we are surely prepared, with Paul, to be servants of others (4:5) with the gospel, for the sake of Jesus. There is no greater privilege than to serve Christ in this way.

4: Home or away 4:7–5:8

The Christian is always in a tension between the now and the future. We have become children of God through faith in Christ Jesus but we are still living in the world. We look forward to the redemption of our bodies but for the moment we still live in them. The captivity of sin over our bodies is broken but the sinful nature is still there. The freedom from pain, sorrow and tears lies ahead in heaven but here we are still very much involved with them. We are citizens of heaven but also citizens of earth. We are pilgrims to the promised land but walk through the heat of the world's desert on the way.

Some Christians want heaven now. They believe in sinless perfection and even bodily wholeness. They want freedom from pain and trouble, believing that all the heavenly promises can be ours now. Others want to withdraw from the world and try to live in separated groups. Paul is a strong antidote to such ideas! He believes in the power of God to change us and to heal. But he never promises total freedom from all sin and all sickness.

Heaven often touches us and thrills us but these experiences are to encourage us on in this earthly pilgrimage. Paul helps us here to come to terms with our humanity and with the glory ahead. He shows us that the Christian way is not to allow one to submerge the other but to hold both together, richly and fully. This is his answer to the false apostles in Corinth who had taught the Corinthians to despise Paul because of the sufferings he was enduring. Their teaching that a real Christianity means freedom from suffering was given from the safety of the fellowship in Corinth. But Paul is out in the world working with courage and fervour for the cause of Christ; he knows the reality of pain, deprivation, danger and persecution (he later lists many of these experiences in Chapter 11:21ff). The successors of the false apostles are still around. See how wrong they are – listen to Paul!

Fragile – handle with care! (4:7)

'We have this treasure in jars of clay.' We can rightly get very excited about the Christian faith. We have been uplifted by Paul in the previous verses so that glory seems only a step away. We can say 'Amen' to his vivid description of the work of the Spirit and of the transforming process taking place in our lives. We can be freshly overwhelmed by the fact that it is the God who created the world who has shone his light into our hearts. We are awed and humbled by the privilege we have, not just to know about Christ but to know him. Yes, this is real Christianity. This is 'treasure'. But we have this treasure in jars of clay. Only in the future will the treasure be in a new res- urrection body and freed from all the trappings of sin. For the moment it is in this earthly frame – this 'jar of clay'.

Jars of clay are commonplace in the east even in this day of plastics and unbreakable materials. There are thousands of clay jars around. They are made cheaply. They are easily breakable. If you squash one, it will break. If you drop one, it will break. Yet it can contain all sorts of things and does so effectively. It is an apt picture of the human body. The potential use of the body is enormous but it is easily breakable. If you squash it, it will break. If you drop it, it will break. It is fragile.

We should accept this fragility and not fight against it. We can do a lot to keep our bodies fit and well. We can develop skills and abilities. Yet we must beware of over-pushing our bodies and thinking that, for instance, because we are in Christ's service, we can do without adequate sleep or relaxation. Jesus knew the need for times apart and times to rest and be refreshed. We should recognize this need too.

A girl came to see me. She was a fine worker in the church and was serving with much energy and faithfulness. However, she began to show signs of strain. She was not sleeping properly. She was 'on edge'. When I talked with her I found that she had no planned relaxation. The Biblical concept of 'redeeming the time' had been interpreted by her as not wasting any time in relaxation. When I explained to her that at the end of the day – when I could get home at around 10 pm – I found it necessary to be unhooked from all the concerns of the day and that often the television was the quickest means of doing this, she was startled. 'You actually watch TV?' she said. This splendid girl had not come to terms with the fragility of her body and when she learnt to relax more she found again her freshness in Christ's service.

There are times when we must shut the door and be alone. At All Souls Langham Place we shut the church down completely in the week after Christmas and all the staff are off. After the enormous pressure through the autumn we believe it to be vital that there is a complete break to refresh us all for the demands of the new year. Complaints come from outsiders but then there are always those who expect us to work all the time and never to relax. We must not be pushed by them.

Fragile but amazingly useful (4:7)

Paul takes the idea of fragility and turns it to positive advantage in the service of Christ. He points out that when the treasure is so evident in the jars of clay that others see it, then the glory is to God. He himself was probably small of stature and nothing to look at. Several times there are allusions to his appearance and manner of speech as if others tended to despise his physical experience. Good! (says Paul) then you can more readily see that all the conversions, missionary successes, churches established in numerous towns and cities, all the survival of long and dangerous journeys, all the power in preaching, is from God and not from me.

A little while ago I was giving the farewell address for a missionary returning to northern India. As I was speaking I was struck afresh by her apparent fragility. She was nothing much to look at and certainly not anyone that you would have given a second glance to in the street. Yet here she was, going back to North India to serve Christ. She had already served there for many years and had done so with amazing courage, enterprise and vision. She would tell of her experiences with a lovely touch of humour that tended to play down the power of what had been happening. Humanly her return would appear a waste of money but again God would use her and work powerfully through her. The glory would be the Lord's.

So it is with all of us. There are not many wise, powerful or of noble birth in the service of Christ. Instead, says Paul in 1 Corinthians 1, God has chosen the foolish to shame the wise, the weak to shame the strong, the low and despised to bring to nothing things that are. And why? 'That no human being may boast in the presence of God.'

Years ago I was an officer at a boys' camp. The team of officers contained some outstanding people – fine athletes, physically strong men and some very intelligent and gifted men from the top universities. The evening talks were taken by each officer in turn. They were usually excellent. Then one night the talk was quite embarrassing. The officer was nervous, hesitant, mixed up his words, stumbled through his talk. In human terms it was a disaster and the rest of us hardly knew where to look during it. Yet that was the night God reached through to the boys. Many of them came to real faith or began to seek earnestly. The 'all-surpassing power' was clearly from God and not from the speaker. God had used the fragility and used it amazingly!

Not exuberance but endurance (4:8–9)

Once we have the principle of verse 7 in our minds we can face life in a different way. We see the experiences of life, the sufferings and the pressures, as opportunities in which to glorify God. We do not spend our time pleading with God to take away all the sufferings and persecutions. If they are removed, that's great! But if not, it is an opportunity for God's power to be shown in our fragility. Paul had this approach written deeply into his whole being. He expresses it vividly in Philippians 1 where he is facing the possibility of imminent martyrdom. His one desire is to glorify Christ whether in the way he dies or in further service in his life on earth.

Here in 2 Corinthians 4 there are four experiences: hard pressed (*thlipsis* again), perplexed, persecuted, struck down. Apart from persecution, they are commonplace to life itself and to all humanity. There is rarely a family that has not experienced problems, pressures, sudden illness and the like. The Christian is not delivered from such things. Some people want to be. How often you hear someone say 'Why has that happened to her? She was such a good Christian.' The popular philosophy is that such things ought not to happen to Christians. If that was the case then everyone would become Christians as an insurance against problems and illness! The Bible view is utterly different. We share these experiences but it is how we handle them that makes the difference.

So we have here 'but not . . . but not . . . but not . . . but not'. This is where the power of Christ enters the scene. We are *not* crushed, nor driven to despair, nor destroyed. In persecution we know we are not abandoned. If we live or die we are the Lord's and we have his power within us. We are sustained by the hope set before us, we are able to come to our Father in prayer, we know that even if men destroy our bodies they cannot destroy our souls. Christ's grace is deeply with us when we are being persecuted for him – as Stephen knew while the crowd was stoning him to death and he could see Jesus 'standing at the right hand of God'.

A beach-hockey game was in vigorous progress during a Christian houseparty. One of the girls playing in it was from the youth group I served as a curate at that time. She had particularly taken Romans 8:28 into her life – that 'all things work together for good for those who love God and are called according to his purpose'. Suddenly, an enthusiastic swing of the hockey stick by another player caught her in the face. Teeth were smashed out, there was blood pouring from her mouth, her lips were swelling like balloons and her face was scarred and bruised. As we rushed her to get medical attention she could hardly speak but just managed to say 'Romans 8:28'! Indeed, that is how it worked out. Several girls came to faith in Christ by seeing how Angela coped with that situation and just recently I met one of those girls, now a mature woman, still growing in Christ. Here was a person 'struck down but not destroyed' and the power of God was a visible witness to others.

We are facing a perplexing challenge, perhaps in our church. We do not know how to tackle what seems to be an impossible situation. Do we sit down and give up? Not if we follow Paul here. Instead we get on our knees and spend time with the Lord. We bring the situation to him. We will go on looking at it from all directions, but all the time will be praying for his way through. There is no despair when Jesus is our Lord. He has a way through for his glory. We must believe that and hold on to that, even when it is a long time before his way is shown. Often there are unseen factors that have to come right before the Lord can open the door for us on this problem. Then when he does open the door we can see the reason for the delay.

The testimonies of those persecuted and imprisoned for Christ are moving to read or hear. The love for their captors, the way in which the presence of the Lord has become so intensely real, the deep work in their soul of knowing him in a new way, the greater and higher hope of life eternal – all these are their testimonies. Peter, in 1 Peter 4, says: 'Rejoice that you participate in the sufferings of Christ, so that you may be over-joyed when his glory is revealed. If you are insulted because of the name of Christ, you are blessed, for the Spirit of glory and of God rests upon you. If you suffer as a Christian, do not be ashamed, but praise God that you bear that name.'

God grant us all the grace to be 'but not' Christians-proving the power and grace of God to be sufficient in the midst of any circumstance that we face in this fallen world.

A matter of life and death (4:10–12)

Elsewhere in the New Testament we are urged to put to death what belongs to our earthly nature and to put on the things of God (Colossians 3). This command springs from the fact that we have died with Christ and are risen again with him.

Here in 2 Corinthians 4 we are urged to let circumstances be a means to that same end. The pressures and perplexities of life are an opportunity to further the death of the old nature and to foster the growth of the new nature; an opportunity to die to self and rise with Christ; an opportunity to know more of the death of Jesus in our beings and to know the life of Jesus too.

Amy Carmichael of Dohnavur had learnt this truth. When wrong things were said about her she regarded the pain as a means to die more to self. The further we go in the Christian life the more we see ourselves as we really are and our desire to die more to self and to be more truly alive in Christ must increase. Here, with Paul, we must learn not to try and sweep the events of life on one side while our 'Christian life' goes on in peace but rather to bring the events of life into the transforming process of our lives. The pruning goes on and on and on. Yet the results of good pruning are seen in greater fruitfulness and more glorious blooms.

Pride will often be a barrier to such a work in our soul. We do not want to lose face with other Christians; we want to appear to others better than we know ourselves to be; we want to hear others say how great we are; we often want to deceive ourselves. Pride has to be broken down before we can open to the transformation of ourselves by life's experiences. It was the breaking of that pride in Peter that brought him to that openness and makes his first letter such a marvellous expression of how to face and use suffering.

Are we prepared to humble ourselves under the mighty hand of God? Are we prepared to let him knock off the sharp corners and work deeply in the festering swamps of our sinful natures? Once I was a choirboy. The choirmaster was keen to improve the voices of another chorister and myself. He asked us to go to his home one evening. When we found out that it was the last evening for seeing a film at the local cinema about a haunted house we were very upset. We went to the choirmaster's house with dragging feet. He was not there when we arrived. Hope sprang in our hearts! Time ticked on. He was delayed at some other meeting. Finally we managed to persuade his wife that he would be very tired when he eventually came home and we ought to go! She let us go. We ran and ran. Our glance down a darkened side street gave us a sight of the choir-master hurrying towards his home – but we were past and rushed on to the cinema for the film (which was terrible!) The real trouble with us was that we did not *want* to have our voices changed and improved. It was not important to us and so lesser things took priority. It is like this in the Christian life. The real question is: Do we *want* to be changed? If so, then we will ponder these verses in 2 Corinthians 4 until they are part of our thinking and thus of our growing in the death and life of Christ. If not, we will be content with lesser things.

Deliverance is also a cause for glory (4:13–15)

As much as Paul sees the value of suffering (both here and in Romans 5: 'Suffering produces perseverance; perseverance, character; and character, hope') he also sees the glory to God in deliverance. He has expressed this in chapter 1 verses 10–11 and does so again here. In the present circumstances he believes God is going to bring about a deliverance which will bring benefit to the Corinthians and cause much thanksgiving. Paul is never in any doubt that God is always able to deliver, to heal, to act in a special way. He believes in the God 'who raised Jesus from the dead'. That same God could raise Paul from his present experience and bring him safely to the Corinthians.

We must not get so carried away with the blessings of suffering, or with the glory to God in enduring pressures and perplexities, that we forget to be open to the possibility of release, healing or restoration. There is a lovely balance in Paul's whole outlook. He wants the glory of God. Because that is his overriding aim he is prepared to let God work out the way in which the glory is to be expressed.

Those who feel that God can only be glorified by total deliverance or healing are obstructing God's purpose. Those who feel there can be no special healing or deliverance are also obstructing God's purposes. The right position is to be open to both in prayer, with faith and submission to God. Like Chrysostom, who endured much persecution, we should say, 'Glory to God in all things. Amen!' When the way is deliverance we can have a great celebration, and thanksgiving can abound to the glory of God (v. 15). We share this when a believer is released from imprisonment for their faith, or someone is healed or a way through a problem is opened up clearly and marvellously by the Lord. Yet we must also praise and thank God for his glory worked out in those who are not released or not healed or who do not have the way opened up clearly – and yet who turn this to God's glory.

An eternal perspective is good for you! (4:16–18)

The old jibe about Christians being so heavenly-minded that they are of no earthly use is easily thrown at us but is easily rebuffed. Of course there are those to whom the criticism is sadly applicable. But for most Christians, being heavenly-minded inspires us to be more useful in this life. The accusation does sometimes make Christians feel a little ashamed of any thoughts about heaven or eternity. If that applies to you then let these verses grip your soul. Paul was constantly inspired by what lay ahead and found great strength from the eternal perspective in his life. It affects all our values, our ambitions, our attitudes – as well as thrilling us!

There are three contrasts here. The first is between the outer and the inner. Our outer fabric, our body, is in irreversible decay! There is no great harm in keeping the decaying work in check wherever possible, in keeping our bodies as pleasant and fit as possible. But all the decoration and jogging and slimming we apply to it is a losing battle. The body is decaying and one day will return to dust.

Yet the real you and the real me can be renewed every day! Although the wrinkles come, the eyesight fades and energy decreases, the soul can keep young and fresh as well as maturing, with ever fresh insight into the things of God and no decrease of inward power.

People without hope in Christ tend to grow old inwardly as well as outwardly, but the Christian has the Holy Spirit within and this means new life day by day. What a lovely thing it is to see true believers in their old age, still eager to learn more of Jesus, still wanting to grow in the knowledge of him and of his word, and with the fruit of the Holy Spirit manifested in their loving lives. I was deeply moved by a group of elderly believers living in the Mowll Retirement Village in Australia. They were at the CMS Summer School where I was speaking. After each session they would come and clutch my hand, tears of gratitude in their eyes, praising God for what they had learned anew that evening in the talk, longing to know more of him. And they were such fun, too!

Not all elderly Christians are like that, and the reason is here in verse 16. The renewal 'day by day' is not automatic. It is true only for those who seek that daily renewal, who feed on the word and learn to meditate, who learn to have devotional prayer fellowship with their Lord day by day, who long to grow in Christ. Whatever our age, this is vital to renewal. Renewal is not something cornered by a movement or a special segment of Christianity. It is the birthright of every believer and is possible and intended for every believer. Don't throw it away by laziness.

The second contrast is between the present light and momentary troubles and the weighty glory of eternity. This life is really very short. Sixty, seventy, eighty years – sometimes more, sometimes less. Nothing when compared with eternity. As Calvin said: 'A moment is long if we look at the things around us, but once we have raised our minds to heaven, a thousand years begin to be like a moment.' There is simply no comparison, says Paul, between the short time in this fallen world and all that God has prepared for those who love him. So whenever the going gets rough, lift your eyes and get a glimpse of glory ahead; stand on your spiritual mountain-top and look across to the mighty peaks of heaven. That is where you are heading, and when you get there the journey back on earth will seem to have been so short, and the things we regarded as great human aims and glories on earth will look so petty and paltry compared with the glory of heaven.

53

The third contrast is between what is seen, which is temporary, and what is unseen, which is eternal. Jesus told us not to lay up treasure on earth but to lay up treasure in heaven. The materialistic world sets great store by wealth, luxury, fame and success. The Christian is influenced by these attitudes all the time and has to work out a lifestyle for living in the world yet preparing for eternity. We are helped by seeing that most of the things the world prizes are temporary and geared only to this world. Yet the true values of life and love, of sharing and caring, of worship and fellowship, are with us for ever. So we must constantly 'fix our eyes' not on the seen but on the unseen. This is not a change of perspective achieved in a moment and then always with us but rather a constant refixing of our eyes, a constant adjustment in our navigating perspective.

You are on your way home (5:1-5)

If your home is really a home then you will always look forward to returning after a journey or even after a holiday. Before the time of our summer holiday we limp towards getting away and then, on holiday, thoroughly enjoy being apart from the pressures of normal working life. But after two or three weeks we begin to look forward to going home. Paul thinks of heaven in those terms. It is not that we will then be away but that we are away now and then will be home (v. 8).

Are you looking forward to 'going home'? Perhaps you are still young and thoughts of eternity are fairly remote. You probably still have much of your life on earth to live; but as you get older the perspective changes.

Paul is enormously confident about the prospect. In 5:1 he says 'we know' (this means it is something we have come to understand and grasp with conviction) and in 5:6 'we are always confident'. The unbeliever will readily chide us for such confidence. We were visiting a family for a meal. During it our youngest, in his early teens at the time, was describing his delight at visiting Disneyland. 'When I get to heaven,' he said, 'I will want to thank Mr. Disney for creating Disneyland.' The mother of the family we were visiting rounded on him and with scorn and acidity mocked him for his confidence about going to heaven. He was startled but unmoved.

The confidence comes, of course, from the promises of God and the resurrection of Jesus. There is, however, a restlessness in the Christian's heart, a sense of anticipation, a feeling that so much more lies ahead, a sense that a far greater life is in store, a longing to have the resurrection body and freedom from this earthly one. This restlessness, this tension between what is and what will be, is a result of the Holy Spirit's indwelling. Indeed, the very restlessness is a sign of the Spirit being within us, for the unspiritual person has no such tension or longing other than a vague hope. If he thinks about heaven it is only as an afterthought to this life and not as the glorious destiny of the redeemed. Bathe in the wonder of verse 5: 'It is God who has made us for this very purpose.' That is our destiny, fellow-believer!

The Holy Spirit is the deposit (v. 5), the down payment, the first instalment, the pledge of what is to come. We touch and experience glory by his indwelling but always knowing that this is but the hem of the garment, the foretaste of the fullness to come.

Home with the Lord

Supremely, going home means going home not to a place but to a person. This is true in human families

– the long-distance telephone calls, the letters, the longing to be reunited with loved ones, the moment of crossing the threshold and being greeted with open arms of love. How much more is that going to be true when we go home to the Lord. At the moment, although we have his indwelling and his presence with us, we are still, in Paul's terms 'away from the Lord' (v. 6). But then, when this earthly life ceases, the earthly body is left behind, the fallen world has dropped away from us, we shall come to him. Whatever heaven may be like (and it will be glorious!) the centre of it all will be the Lord himself. We shall be at home with the Lord, and with all who love him, for ever!

5: Ambassador or passenger? 5:9–6:13

The flame of eternal hope has been fanned into a blazing fire in the verses we have been studying. Glory filled the horizon. Without any apology, Paul encouraged us to revel in what lies ahead and all that it will mean to be 'at home with the Lord'.

Now, suddenly, the prospect of heaven ahead is applied to service in the present. Not only will we come into our heavenly inheritance, but we will come before Christ with the life he gave us to live for him on earth. It will be a time for reporting back and for looking at what we have done for him. Paul now develops this theme into a major attack upon the Corinthians' lack of evangelistic concern and urges them, with the flowing passion of a heart committed to evangelism, to get into action, regardless of possible persecution and physical hardship. They are to prove themselves as genuine servants of God.

Goal! (v. 9)

What is the greatest goal, ambition, aim of your life? Paul has one supreme goal – to please Christ. This will be his aim when he is at home with the Lord and it is his ambition while he is still away from the Lord. The thin line between life on earth and life in heaven is no interruption to this overriding ambition.

Does this mean that we cannot have other ambitions in life? Is it wrong to want to win at sport or to succeed in examinations or to get promotion in our job? Not at all. It is great to have Christians in positions of success and influence as this can often be effectively used for Christ. Yet if such positions are what we most want in life we have got it wrong. Success will carry with it responsibility to others but particularly to God. His glory is to be our supreme aim and it is often more difficult to let this be seen and worked out when we are in success situations.

Earthly ambitions are fine as long as they are submitted at the feet of Christ. It is in such submission that we often find Christ requiring us to take a role that may never appear successful in human terms, to go across the world and to serve in some obscure yet needy area, to be 'behind the scenes' in some work for him and never hitting the headlines. Are we prepared for Christ to show us such spheres as his ambition for us? If we are, then we can handle human ambitions of any kind because over and above them will be the ambition to please him.

The goal is personal. It is to please him. Our Lord and our Saviour has done and continues to do so much for us. The only logical response to his mercy and love is in the surrender of our lives – to give back our bodies to him as a living sacrifice (Romans 12:1–2), not to a 'cause' but to a person. When I was called into the Army at eighteen I was sent first to a training camp in the north of England. At first we all resented the discipline and the constant shouting of orders. Then we were transferred to another section and placed under an Irish sergeant-major. He immediately won our love and respect. He was a wonderful man and, when it came to the passing-out parade, every soldier on the barrack square wanted it to be perfect – for him. They did not want to let him down and so, when at one point the howling wind prevented many hearing the order to 'about turn' and half the troop went one way and half the other way, we were all terribly upset. We had let him down, this sergeant-major who meant so much to us. We had no ambition to present a perfect passing-out parade for its own sake – but we did for his sake.

In the same way, the living of a life of love and service for its own sake – or to fulfil a standard of law – is not likely to inspire us. But living a life of love and service for Christ, who has saved us and loves us, transforms the situation. When we fail, we let him down. When we do not bother to serve, we grieve his heart. When we are in action under his direction we bring joy to his heart.

I find this a great encouragement and corrective. Often I feel that it would be good to do some other job, or to have the opportunity to have a different sort of ministry, or to achieve what some others achieve, or to have different gifts to use, or to be in a different place and a different sphere. But then I am recalled to the fact that I am the servant of Christ and my greatest aim is to be where he wants me to be, to do what he wants me to do, when he wants me to do it.

Criticism is always hard to take, particularly if we are sensitive. We are told that we should be doing this or doing that, or that we should be exercising this gift or that ministry, or that we should not be doing things in this particular way, or that the way the church is tackling the local area is not how it should be done and some other church is uplifted as the pattern. We cannot reject criticism. We must weigh it. But in the end we are answerable to God. We have to be God-pleasers not man-pleasers. We must be fully persuaded in our own minds that the course of action, the form of ministry, the strategic plan, is the

Lord's and we must not be swayed from it by the extolling of what happens elsewhere. Christ is the head of the Church and our ambition must be to please him.

The judgement-seat (vs. 10–13)

The judgement seat of Christ is here the judging-place of Christians. It is not the judgement over eternal salvation. That is an issue settled by our faith in Christ as Saviour. Paul is in no doubt about that, as the rest of this chapter shows (v. 19).

If you find this idea confusing then turn back to 1 Corinthians 3:11–15. There Paul makes it clear that there is only one foundation and that is Jesus Christ. That foundation stands all the tests and if we are on that foundation we are on it for ever. However, what we build on the foundation is going to be tested as by fire. He contrasts the lasting value of gold, silver and precious stones with the short-lived wood, hay or straw. What will be tested in the Day of the Lord will be the quality of our work for Christ, says Paul. Will it survive the test because it has been really worthwhile or will it disappear in smoke because it has been useless and shallow? It is a sombre and challenging contrast to ponder. 1 Corinthians 3:15 then makes sure we do not get the salvation implication wrong. If our work is burned up we will suffer loss but we 'will be saved'. So the judgement seat, before which 'we must all appear' (2 Corinthians 5:10) – and that has the implication of everything being in the open – is concerned with how we have built on the foundation. It is concerned with our life since we became part of his family through faith.

Christ will look at our lives in practical terms. It will be about 'things done while in the body' (v. 10). It is the body that acts, serves, sits with the ill, visits the prisoners, scrubs floors, cooks meals, moves chairs, cares for the elderly, makes coffee, provides hospitality, befriends the outcast, runs camps, goes across the world or the street or the corridor to serve others. It is the body that is to be a clean vessel for Christ to use, not caught up with the world's marring and lowering of the image of God in man, nor involved in bestiality, sadism, cruelty, promiscuity and the like. It is with the body that we think, study, speak and converse. It is with the body that we can be helpful or hurtful. It is with the body that we serve Christ now.

Although every believer will share in salvation and thus in eternal life there is clearly a differential made in the recognition by Christ of what has or has not been done for him. Jesus indicated this in his parable of the talents. However, whatever form this may take, there is no doubt that our joy or shame before Christ will be the primary response in our hearts. His 'Well done, good and faithful servant' will be worth everything – all the years of service and action for him. His disappointment at our failure to use our life fruitfully for him will be like a stab-wound – we will wish that we could go back and re-live our lives. It will be too late then, so learn the lesson now. Aim for the crown. Aim to run so that you may win.

Paul responds on his own part by fresh zeal in evangelism. When he speaks of the fear of the Lord (verse 11) causing him to try and persuade others with the gospel, he is not thinking of their judgement but of his own. He uses 'fear' in the sense of 'awe'. There is indeed a great awesomeness about our facing Christ and we should never treat it lightly. Nor should we treat service for Christ lightly or casually. I find the pulpit a place of awe and joy. I was rapidly delivered from the fear of faces and from fear of preaching to large crowds. The vast congregations at All Souls soon did not worry me. Yet I have become increasingly burdened with the awe of God, the awe of handling his word and being the messenger of God to so many people. I do not want to let him down and I find it hard to get peace with myself if I feel I have not handled the word as well as he wanted and as well as I ought to have done.

What is true of the pulpit is true of any sphere of service for him – we must not be casual about preparation for a Sunday School class, a Bible study group, organizing visitation, counselling, even in the many practical tasks of Christian service, in the kitchen or maintaining premises or participation in committees.

We must also beware of judging others by what is seen. The Corinthians did that (v. 12) and apparently formed a wrong judgement. In the final analysis it is God who judges perfectly as he sees the heart. Be encouraged by that if you find yourself wrongly judged by others: 'What we are is plain to God' (v. 11). Even if (v. 13) others think us out of our mind in our service for Christ (Jesus' relatives thought this about him and often our friends and relatives think it about us) Paul does not swerve because, he says in a neat turn of phrase, 'if we are out of our mind it is for the sake of God'!

Love is compelling (vs. 13–15)

Action is stirred by the thought of Christ's judgement seat; it is compelled by the thought of Christ's love. Paul is not referring to our love for Christ but to Christ's love for us. It is the *agape* of God that is central here. There is a form of love for Christ that is sustained by fresh fervour in rallies, meetings and services – it needs to be worked up and maintained constantly. Those who depend on this get into depression when they do not feel that love and go into spiritual 'highs' when they do feel it. They tend to go up and down in their spiritual state.

Stability only comes when we see it the other way round. Christ's love for us is a fact – a fact of history and a fact of our personal history if we have believed on him. The fact of the cross will never alter. It will be a fact tomorrow and the next day and the next day . . . and for ever. What God intends is that every believer should more and more deeply understand the meaning of the cross and thus of his love for us. Romans 5:5 confirms this: 'God has poured out his love into our hearts by the Holy Spirit.' It is his love for us that the Holy Spirit wants us to understand and experience. The Holy Spirit is the agent of making this love in the cross more real to us.

The cross is at the centre of Paul's heart. He has pondered long and deep on the significance of Christ's crucifixion and the Holy Spirit has been his illuminator. It comes out time and time again in his letters. We must ponder the cross too. Like Paul, we must be 'convinced that one died for all'. The word 'convinced' means something that is thought through. The tense in which it is expressed means that it is not a developing idea but a conviction firmly established and influencing our whole life.

There are those who teach that the cross is supremely an example of God's love to inspire us; or that it is the supreme evidence of what evil wants to do to good. Both these ideas are helpful but neither is the major meaning of the cross in the Bible. There is overwhelming biblical testimony to the cross being supremely God taking our place and taking the penalty we deserve as sinners. So here: 'one died for all'. It is technically known as 'substitutionary atonement'. Do not be put off by those who call this a barbaric theory or a heathen idea. They are attacking a warped version of substitution and not the biblical one. And

63

they miss so much! Unless you and I have grasped the truth of Christ's dying in our place we can never know real assurance of salvation. You will observe that those who try to discredit substitutionary atonement also discredit the idea of man being able to have assurance of salvation. The two are linked together.

A clergyman I knew once brought the issue to a sharp head in his church by saying in the middle of his sermon: 'Stand up if you know you are saved.' There was an enormous furore afterwards. 'How dare those people stand up – the presumptuousness of saying they are saved – nobody can know that until the day of judgement.' I knew how they felt as I had thought like that myself. There was no lack of sincerity in what they were saying. Yet, of course, they were missing the point, as I had done for so many years. Those who say they are saved are not doing so because they think they are good enough for God (the force of the 'presumptuousness' jibe) but because they do not think they can ever be good enough for God. Their trust is in Jesus Christ as dying for them, taking the penalty of their sin and declaring them his children for ever.

The 'presumptuous' people are actually those who reckon that in the day of judgement they will be all right because they will have lived lives good enough for God. Their trust is in themselves, not in the Saviour of the world. They see their so-called good deeds as their passport to heaven. Because they do not see themselves as lost sinners they do not see the point or need of Christ dying in their place on the cross.

This is the most important issue for any human being and so I want to ask you straight: where is your trust for salvation? Is it in Jesus or yourself? Do you really believe that he died for you and that therefore you have died and been raised to new life in Christ? He died for all, says Paul – for everyone in the world, in every generation. No one is excluded from the possibility of salvation. 'Therefore all died' means that Christ died as the representative of the whole human race. There is no universalism here of everyone being saved but only of the offer of salvation being universal. We must receive and believe to make it our own.

Vital as this truth is to grasp and ponder, the point of Paul declaring it here is as a spur to evangelism and service for Christ. There is a compulsion. 'Christ's love compels us.' The word means a holding together, a pressing together, a hemming in. The late Alan Stibbs, in expounding this verse, would illustrate it by his experience travelling by boat along a Chinese river. The river was sluggish as it went across the flat plains but then it came to a narrow gorge. The waters tumbled and roared with great force so that the passengers had to hold on tightly. The power came when the waters were hemmed in, said Alan Stibbs. So in the Christian life it is only as our hearts and lives are hemmed in by the love of Christ on the cross that we begin to have real power in service. We are left no choice. The compulsion is such that 'those who live should no longer live for themselves but for him who died for them and was raised again' (v. 15). A revolution takes place!

Do you find this true in your own life? Perhaps our commitment to Christ's service becomes listless and casual and we live more for ourselves, for our pleasure and our own profit. Then we come to a worship service, especially the communion service, in which the cross is central. Pondering the cross afresh becomes a searchlight to our soul and compels us to rededicate our souls and bodies as a living sacrifice in Christ's service. The cross constantly challenges the bias we have towards living for self and it inspires to a bold and vigorous living for Christ.

New birth has surprising effects! (vs. 16–17)

The text 'if anyone is in Christ he is a new creation' is frequently quoted out of context. The dynamic truth it expresses is taught in many other parts of the Bible and we know its meaning in our lives, for the Holy Spirit brought us to re-birth and has begun to change us. But the reason for stating this truth here is again as an incentive to evangelism and service for Christ.

Look back at verse 16 and you will see two effects of this new creation. The first effect is that 'from now on we regard no one from a worldly point of view'. Before we came to Christ we probably judged people from a 'worldly point of view'. We judged by outward success, intelligence, physique, position, wealth and achievement. Then, when we came to Christ, we found ourselves beginning to see people differently. We began to see through the masks and the plastic exteriors and to see into the heart of people. The Lord always looks on the heart and not at the outward appearance. Now the Holy Spirit is helping us to see as he sees. The wealthy executive wielding power but with no peace or deep purpose for living becomes someone to pity and to reach for Christ. The pop star whose music is fantastic, whose skill with the guitar is marvellous, whose records sell in millions and before whom the fans go wild with frenzied adoration, and yet who is desperately lonely, sick of luxury, consumed by drugs and tries to take his own life is to be pitied. He needs Christ. Life is meaningless without Christ. All the riches and fame this world can load upon man can never satisfy the human heart.

So the 'new creation' believer finds himself looking through the façade of lives. He finds himself looking at his relatives in a new light. Though they may be a wonderful family yet if they are without Christ, he cannot but he concerned to pray, love and witness. As we mix with crowds of people day by day we cannot but see them as Jesus did, as 'sheep without a shepherd'. At the same time, the prejudices and barriers should be breaking down. The Christ who has broken the barriers between Jew and Gentile, slave and free, male and female, is the Christ who does not see the colour of the skin or the cultural background of a person. Nor should we. The new creation should help us see other people as he sees them and not from a worldly point of view.

The second effect is that we see Christ differently. Verse 16: 'Though we once regarded Christ in this way, we do so no longer.' In what way? From a 'worldly point of view', which means regarding him just as a man, possibly a very special man but just a man. The effect of the new creation in us is to see Christ as Lord and God, as head of creation and head of the church, as Saviour of the world, as eternal King.

Over a period of a year or so I corresponded with a girl who had written after a world broadcast service. She had rejected Jesus Christ and the Christian faith but gradually by correspondence and reading books she came into a real faith. After a while she wrote this: 'That I could ever have dared to approach God as "some vague abstract higher intelligence", seeking his voice and guidance while simultaneously denying Jesus as Lord and Saviour together with his gospel of love, is much too painful and distressing to verbalise.' No doubt about the new creation happening in her life! She now saw Jesus in an entirely different way.

The reverse of this is true too. There are various theologians and other writers who have written books denying the divinity of Christ. They are sincere in what they are doing but the sad fact is that they are also showing that they have not met with Jesus nor experienced his new creation. They are outside and so can only see Christ from a 'wordly point of view'.

These two changes in our thinking – about other people and about Christ – are further spurs to get on with serving him. There is a great need to reach people everywhere. What we bring them is not a human theory but a gospel made possible through the eternal Son of God himself. We know it to be true because we experience this new creation. 'The old has gone, the new has come'!

God is relying on you (5:18–21)

God has entrusted something to you and to me: 'he has committed to us the message of reconciliation' (v. 19). Nobody else can do it for him. Only believers, who themselves have received this reconciliation, this salvation, can possibly share it with others. So God relies on each of us to get on with the task for him. No angels will preach to your neighbour, no seraphic choir will announce it to your colleagues at work, no vision in the sky will declare it to your relatives and friends. The message now has to come through human agency – through you and me, through all of us who are 'in Christ'.

The title of 'ambassadors' is given to us (v. 20). What a title! Quite often, in the area of London in which I lived, I saw the ambassadors of foreign countries setting off in the ceremonial coach to present their credentials to the sovereign. The ambassador speaks for his country and for the leader of his country. He does not speak on his own behalf. So when we act as ambassadors for Christ we speak in his name and not in our own name. It is (v. 20) 'as though God were making his appeal through us' . . . 'we implore on Christ's behalf'. There is, incidentally, no 'you' in the Greek. It is important to see that Paul is not pleading with the Corinthians to be reconciled, for they had already received Christ; rather, he is showing that the task of the ambassador is to implore others to be reconciled.

The content of our message is that the reconciliation has taken place in Christ, dealing with the sins of mankind. We are to declare that this has happened and then to urge others to accept it: 'Be reconciled to God.' It has to be received. We cannot reconcile ourselves but we are to 'be reconciled'. In humility we receive what he has done once and for all.

We need also to show how this was made possible – through Christ alone and what he did. Verse 21 has been described as the most profound verse in the Bible. It gets to the heart of substitutionary atonement. It is not just bearing sins but that he became sin. We can only stand in awe on the edge of this truth, hearing the cry from the cross, 'My God, my God, why have you forsaken me?' and sensing something of the awful darkness that came upon Jesus in that terrible separation from the Father. Our wonder at this divine love is made greater when we see here again that he who became sin was himself without sin. There could be no greater contrast. We whose attitude to sin is often blurred can hardly appreciate what it meant for Christ the sinless to become sin. Stand with awe and heartfelt adoration before the truth of this verse. This is love amazing, and love that had as its aim making us right with God. The reconciliation was made possible through Christ's once-and-for-all sacrifice. We who have received its salvation can surely have no greater privilege or expression of our thanksgiving than to be ambassadors for him with this glorious gospel of reconciliation.

Is God's grace in vain? (6:1–13)

After those closing verses of chapter 5 it seems impossible for Christians ever to grow slack in their desire to reach others with the loving reconciliation of Christ. Yet when we look into our own hearts we know it can be so. It was certainly true of the Corinthians. They had become so turned in on themselves with their spiritual self-indulgence that evangelism had become of little importance. Hence, Paul's driving force of argument throughout chapter 5, which contains some of the greatest truths of scripture concerning the cross, but which is aimed most of all at stirring the Corinthians into action.

Now comes Paul's final plea on this theme. He urges them 'not to receive God's grace in vain'. So this is not a plea to receive Christ, but rather a plea to them as believers not to sit back and do nothing about it. The words of verse 2 are often used as an evangelistic appeal: 'Now is the time of God's favour, now is the day of salvation.' But their purpose is to stir the Corinthians to get on with spreading the gospel. It seems possible that they might have been saying, 'Well, let's enjoy and deepen our fellowship first and then we may think about evangelism.' Paul says the time is always now for evangelism, not tomorrow or the next day – today is always the day. He is urging them not to throw away the opportunities of the present moment.

What else can he say to them? He has pointed them to the judgement seat of Christ, to the compelling love of Christ, to their new attitude to people and to the expectation of Christ for all of us to be ambassadors. His final thrust is by pointing to himself and those with him, to show what it means to serve Christ. He knows that the Corinthians will be told by the false apostles that all this is the energy of the flesh and human effort rather than God's way. There is a sense of 'Well, here I go anyway, whatever you think – listen to this. . . !'

So he plunges into this cascading flow of events and experiences, piling one upon another with breathless rapidity and leaving us with the unmistakable impression that here is a man on fire for God.

Before he lists the activities he shows us his concern not to be a stumbling block to others. That is a sharp warning. Many stories can be told of those who became so busy for Christ that their own spiritual growth stopped and they began to wither inwardly until their life became a barrier to the gospel. The 'discrediting' of our ministry he refers to in verse 3 is a mocking, a ridicule, a despising of any disparity between word and life. As Denney put it: 'People will be glad of an excuse not to listen to the gospel and will look for such in the conduct of ministers.' Or Calvin: 'It is an artifice of Satan to seek some misconduct on the part of ministers which may tend to the dishonour of the gospel.' This applies to all who will be ambassadors for Christ. We cannot always avoid the bitter and ugly defamations or distorted condemnations that come; Jesus experienced such himself. But we can do our best to avoid what might give rise to such attacks.

In the list from verses 4–10 the overall quality shown is endurance – 'stickability'. The fire of the ambassador's heart is not extinguished by anything thrown at him or poured over him. Paul pressed on regardless of the opposition. He did not keep inside a cosy fellowship circle and do nothing.

It is possible to categorise the list to help us apply it to our own lives:

1. Things that happen to us as they do to anybody in the world – the troubles (yes, our old friend *thlipsis* again), the hardships of poverty, illness, unemploy-

ment, the 'distresses' of perplexity, sudden bereavement. All these, as we saw earlier in this letter, are opportunities to be an ambassador of the grace of Christ.

2. The things we may go through, simply because we are Christians. For Paul, there were the beatings, imprisonments and riots. He certainly went through some terrible experiences. So have countless thousands of Christians through the centuries, in the cause of the gospel.

3. Things that we cause ourselves by our work for the gospel. For Paul: 'hard work, sleepless nights, hunger'. Once we have ambassadorship for Christ in our blood we will go to great lengths to serve, and being a committed Christian is very hard work and long hours!

4. The fruit of the Spirit in action in our daily lives: patience, love, truth, power, not being sunk by the fickle opinions of others.

5. The spiritual alchemy that transforms situations by the power of Christ. We may be regarded as people not worth knowing but we are sure the Lord knows us; we are dead and useless in the eyes of the swinging society around us but we know real life in Christ; we will not let our spirit be killed even though our body is beaten; we find joy in Christ as well as sorrow for the world; we are poor perhaps yet possessing everything! What a testimony! Paul certainly lived his life in the triumphant grace of Christ – and he lived it in out-and-out service for Christ.

So can the Corinthians still remain unmoved? Do they still close their heart to Paul, as the false apostles had influenced them to do? Could they still write him off? In spite of all the pain he feels, he loves them and has opened his heart wide to them. He longs that they might open wide their hearts too.

6: Godly separation and godly sorrow 6:14–7:16

1. *Godly separation*

The issue to grasp. The verses between chapter 6 verse
14 and chapter 7 verse 1 must be among the most
misused in the Bible. They seem to form a segment
of their own and some people think they are part of
the letter referred to in 1 Corinthians 5.9. Whether
this is so or not does not affect the truth being com-
municated, which is a strong statement on 'separation'. It has been used by some as a reason for
retreating away from all other people into remote com-
munities, or for separation even from other Christian
groups who do not line up with what is considered
necessary for the Christian life. Families have been
broken up and friendships marred by a legalistic use
of this passage. Yet is is certainly a passage to ponder
deeply and we cannot treat it idly.

It has to be seen in the context of our Lord's re-
quirements in John 17 that his disciples should be 'in
the world but not of the world'. The fact of Christ
becoming man – the Incarnation – implies a sharing
in human life and not a separation from it. Yet, at the
same time, the one who so readily ate with tax-collec-
tors and sinners showed us also how to be separated
to God and to keep close to the Father. As we look
at Jesus we realize that he did not make *deep* bonds

of relationship with unbelievers even though he mixed freely with them and spoke to them of the faith. Similarly, in the verses before us here we can see that it is *deep* bonds, permanent or semi-permanent relationships, which Paul is describing. He uses the word 'yoked' and the picture is of two animals joined together in the task of pulling a plough or a cart so that they have to keep closely in step and be closely identified in a common task and purpose. It is not two animals having a chat in a field!

The inequality. Paul suggests inequality with this picture of two animals entirely unsuited to each other yet yoked together. He may have visualized one animal much taller than the other or he may have recalled Deuteronomy 22:10 where the yoking of an ox and a donkey is forbidden. He is demonstrating the fact that there is a total inequality between an unbeliever and a believer if they are in a close personal bond. He goes on to describe righteousness and wickedness as utterly opposite to each other. They cannot mix as they are on entirely different planes of thought and action. You cannot mix light and darkness. Either you have dark or you have light – the in-between twilight is neither one thing nor the other. If you try to mix them one of them becomes dominant. In Ephesians 5.8 Paul tells us that when we are light in the Lord we should not only *avoid* darkness but *expose* the works of darkness. The two are at war and no compromise can be contemplated. The point is now pressed further by contrasting Christ and Belial – (Belial is usually equivalent to Satan although it means 'worthless'). How can there be a mixing here? How can someone under bondage to Satan mix with someone under the lordship of Christ? As Jesus said: 'No man can serve two masters.'

It is this argument of the total incompatibility or

inequality that we have to take into our thinking. It is obviously referring to close liaisons and committed relationships rather than to casual acquaintances. So it seems perfectly justified to apply this passage to marriage, business partnerships, close friendships and employment. Often when I find myself counselling a Christian and a non-Christian who want to get married, I find they regard the spiritual aspect as of secondary importance. 'Yes, she can go to church and, yes, she can send the children to Sunday School, and, yes, she can take an interest in Christian things if she wants to . . .' as if it was all a matter of taste or fashion. Yet the issue is far deeper. When a person turns to Christ his whole life and outlook are changed and will go on being transformed. A marriage to a non-Christian will produce endless clashes on the ambitions of life, on the use of time and money, on ethical actions, on honesty and truth, on the way Sunday is observed, on facing matters with or without prayer, on the use of the home, and on how the children are brought up. The differences are in the foundations; the Christian will be guided by the authority of the Word of God and the non-Christian by personal opinions, or humanistic philosophies or by selfish motives.

Of course, there are exceptions to this and sometimes there are splendid results in the non-Christian partner coming into a real faith in Christ. But there are more disasters than successes, as usually the Christian is forced to compromise time after time and eventually loses the vitality of faith in the living God. The warning of scripture and experience should be heeded by those contemplating a marriage that is 'mixed' in the matter of faith. Both parties will be wounded, not just the believer.

In the world of commerce or at the local level of being an employee, the warning of this passage must also be heeded. A Christian may find himself forced to share in a dishonest act, perhaps day by day. One Christian I know was working for a brewery when he came to faith. It was regular custom to handle one barrel a day dishonestly – to falsify records and to pocket the money. When he became a Christian, he refused to do this and no-one would go on the lorry with him. He was forced to change his job. Another Christian was involved, before coming to faith, in insurance swindles, arranging for flood damage to 'happen' to stock that could no longer be sold. He refused to do this when he became a Christian and his employers reacted strongly. The ethics of business are sometimes – often – regarded as different from any other ethics and so when a Christian applies the un-changing ethical standards of the Bible he is not wel-come. So avoid close business liaisons which are 'unequal yoking'. Differences, in marriage or other close relationships, over tastes, sports, colour schemes, food and the like are of secondary import-ance – they are areas of give and take. But the issues of the Spirit and of submission to Jesus Christ are not negotiable. Inequality at this level is a recipe for disaster.

The indwelling. Next, Paul drives home the fact that we are temples of the living God. In 1 Corinthians 3.16, he had spoken of our bodies as temples and said that God's Spirit lives in us. Just as in Old Testament times there could be no compromise between heathen idols and the temple of God, so it is with us. Idols were lifeless, not hearing, not seeing, not walking (Psalm 115) and were the works of men's hands; but the living God is over all and does what he pleases. If we play around with heathen philosophies or the materialistic gods of our modern world, we are dis-honouring the living God whose we are and who indwells us by his Spirit. The thought is almost unthinkable.

The promise that God would live with us and walk among us has now been fulfilled in Christ and by the Spirit. No other idols can be given house-room. A close liaison – a yoked partnership – with an unbeliever (who is not in Christ) is seen as compromise and as a rival to the lordship of Christ within us. Who is Lord? Who is in charge of our lives? We have to ask ourselves this constantly. When we find even a friendship pulling us away, challenging Christ, exercising influence in a non-Christian way, involving us in actions, standards or gatherings that are clearly anti-Christ or against His word, it is time to run. We need to break free, to come out and be separate. Equally, where we are able to maintain relationships with unbelievers without compromise or threat to the Lordship of Christ we should do so for the gospel's sake. Sense what is happening and judge what to do. I admire the many Christians who have developed discernment in knowing when to go on cultivating friendships with unbelievers and when to pull out.

The implications. Chapter 7 verse 1 underlines that it is reverence for God which is at stake. Nothing must rival him and our submission to Him. There are two parts to this verse and the first is about specific matters and specific occasions. 'Let us purify ourselves' is in a form of Greek that shows Paul to mean an act of 'purifying' happening many times as we meet each particular challenge. So perhaps we find ourselves in a party that we thought was going to be great but gradually we realize it is an impure gathering and that what is happening is increasingly against the Word and the will of Christ. We must 'purify ourselves' by leaving the party there and then. We have longed for marriage and at first the girl we meet seems wonderful. People think of us as 'a couple' but then we begin to find out things about her that are anything but Christian. Will our pride allow us to pull out? Paul here urges us to do so. Thus with any relationship that goes out of tune spiritually, 'purify' means 'act'.

The other half of the verse is in a form that indicates an on-going effect – a life-time attitude which is steadily deepened and matured by the Spirit. It is the desire to grow in holiness – that is, in reverence for God in our whole life – and it is fed by the word, by prayer, by fellowship, by sharing in the life of the church and by meditating on God and all He has done for us. It is that overriding ambition to be more like Christ and to 'mean business for God' in this world.

If we want to be the best for God then we shall want to avoid all 'that contaminates body and spirit'. The promise in the last verse of chapter 6, itself one of a series of Old Testament references, is that he 'will receive' us and 'be a Father' to us. The testimony of hundreds of thousands of Christians across the centuries would witness to the truth of that promise, that as we draw closer to him so he draws closer to us. What a reward!

2. *Godly Sorrow*

Get loving! The new commandment of Jesus was to love one another so that all men would know that we were his disciples. It is patently true that the amazing bonding-together of all sorts and conditions of people into a fellowship of love is inexplicable humanly. It is always a testimony of the work of the Spirit of God. The power of such testimony is not just quenched if we do not love one another. It actually has the opposite effect! The unbeliever is confirmed in his unbelief and in his cynicism towards the Christian's claims of new life.

So Paul is deeply concerned to see love flowing between Christians and feels deeply about the rift that occurred between himself and the Corinthians. It hurts him that their hearts seem to be closed or at least only partially open towards him. There is no doubt that his is wide open towards them. Back in chapter 6 verses 11–13 he has told them how he is not withholding his affection for them and pleads with them to open their hearts also. Now he again tells them here in chapter 7 verse 3 that they have such a place in his heart that he would live or die with them. His love is like that of a father, for it includes (verse 4) having great confidence in them and pride in them.

He goes on to tell them in verses 5–7 how he longed for news of their response to his earlier letter and of how his joy was 'greater than ever' when Titus came with the good news of their sorrow and concern. But, notice, there is no mention of their love. In spite of their godly sorrow and the good results of the letter, Paul longs for what every Christian should be able to have from fellow Christians: love. Chrysostom says that as heat makes things expand, so the warmth of love will expand a man's heart. Their hearts needed opening. Sad, isn't it? Yet how sad in the present day when you meet someone who is a Christian and yet seems to have a closed heart – a coldness, a defence against love and a Christian life that lacks the overflow of love towards others. Like Paul, we must work to help unblock love's floodgates in such a person. It may mean challenging the falsities that have helped to form a block, as Paul tries to do in chapter 7 verse 2 in exposing the false tongues that had accused him of wrong, corruption and exploitation. It may be in pleading from the heart as he does so well here.

When sorrow is good. Sorrow can be terribly destructive. It can bring bitterness, self-pity and depression.

It can cause despair, anger and self-justification. We can see black as white and white as black in order to justify ourselves. Here Paul speaks of a different sort of sorrow (7:8–11). It is called 'godly sorrow'. Paul says he is *happy* that the Corinthians have had such sorrow.

The difference from ordinary sorrow is in its results. 'Godly sorrow brings repentance that leads to salvation and leaves no regret, but worldly sorrow brings death' (verse 10). The way back from sin is via repentance and this leads to God's forgiveness and His wiping away the sinfulness. Instead of staying in the cloud we come out into the sunshine. In the Corinthians the godly sorrow produced 'earnestness, eagerness to clear themselves, indignation, alarm, longing, concern and readiness to see justice done'. This is an explosive result! It shows us so clearly what repentance is – that it is not just saying 'sorry' but always incorporates a change of attitude, a different way of thinking and an action to put things right wherever possible.

It was such a splendid result that Paul goes as far as saying that his 'painful' letter had the greater purpose, in God's intention, of producing such a result in the Corinthians. It could not be seen just as a correction of the wrongdoer or taking the side of the injured party. It is one of the surprises of Christian experience that we can later often see a higher purpose than the one close at hand, in circumstances and events. It may be a stimulus to faith in the face of deep testing, or a new depth of prayer in facing the impossible, or a new standard of sacrificial giving for the whole of life arising from one 'faith' project involving special giving. So here it has produced a resurrection of the devotion they once had for Paul.

Repentance means action. David's psalm of repentance

(Psalm 51) is a classic example of the good results of godly sorrow. It has been an encouragement to believers down the ages and is a psalm to which many turn in times of failure or sin, when repentance is necessary. If you have never woken up to that psalm I hope you will turn to it now and read it. Then you will have it in your memory as a resource of spiritual help if you come to an incident in your life needing godly sorrow and repentance.

The early church took repentance seriously and often required outward evidence of genuine sorrow and of turning back to God. One such incident was when Bishop Ambrose required repentance of the Emperor Theodosius after the latter had massacred people as a reprisal. Ambrose forbade him Holy Communion for eight months and then the Emperor had to lie on the floor in sackcloth and promise that he would never carry out any further acts of capital punishment without a lapse of thirty days to think about it. The Emperor submitted to this public repentance.

When we are convicted of sin against the Lord and others, the quicker we turn to godly sorrow and repentance the better. Although it is humbling (though seldom as much as it was for Emperor Theodosius!) it is the immediate way back into fellowship with God and with our neighbour. The results will go far further than merely putting things right. God will use the repentance to his glory.

But – love. So Paul was encouraged (verse 13) and the Titus that returned was not just a reporter of what had happened but a Titus refreshed in his spirit. In spite of the problems that had occurred earlier, the Corinthians were still truly the Lord's. Instead of their receiving Titus with antagonism and deaf ears they had welcomed him 'with fear and trembling' (verse 15). This had opened Titus's heart towards them and he now held them in great affection.

But, still, there is one word missing in describing the Corinthians: love. In spite of all the good results from godly sorrow, there is no mention of their love for Paul. He can have 'complete confidence' in them (verse 16) but the crowning joy for Paul would be if they made room in their hearts for him, if they opened wide their hearts to him and if they stopped withholding their affection from him. As he said to them in his first letter: 'If I do not have love, I am nothing.' The Corinthians were slow learners in the school of Christ's love. Are you?

7: 'Generous or stingy?'
Chapters 8 and 9

The big jump

There is an amazing divide between the givers and the non-givers. Whenever I preach on giving I see numbers of people set their jaw, fold their arms and determine not to be affected by the sermon! It is not true that normally there is a steady graph in the Christian's life of starting to give and gradually getting more generous and realistic in giving. Rather, there seems to be a jump between the Christians who live in the shallow water of giving and those who are into it up to their necks. The jump is often sudden but it usually comes only after a considerable battering on our defences. We defend our 'rights' to keep what we have and even when we make good resolves to overhaul our giving we often do not keep the resolve. However, once the revolution has happened it is with us for life and much money is then released for the service of Christ.

Dragging feet

The reluctance to give is nothing new! It is in the heart of man and the last place to get converted, when we come to Christ, is usually our wallet or handbag. The Corinthians were appallingly bad givers. They were full of themselves, thinking what splendid Christians they were, but Paul now ruthlessly exposes them on the matter of giving. What we have here in chapters 8 and 9 is the greatest challenge on giving in the whole of the Bible. If you will face up to it seriously it will (if it has not done so already) create a revolution in your giving. It pulls no punches. It is forceful and unanswerable in its powerful argument. It piles point upon point to break through our defences. It leaves us with only one way to respond!

Me first

First, then, Paul tackles the Corinthians' reluctance to give. There are some lovely Christians who say, 'If you do God's work in God's way He will provide'. That is only part of the picture. It does not allow for human selfishness. As Malachi 3 shows us, the blessing God wants to pour out is often held back because of the selfishness of his people. That selfishness needs to be challenged by preaching and teaching on giving.

But I'm not well off

Paul pricks their self-satisfied consciences by lifting up before them the Macedonian churches. When you think you are 'the tops' and the greatest Christians around, it is singularly irritating to be shown others who are more truly living for Christ. Paul intends them to feel it! The Macedonian churches had shown 'rich generosity' (v. 2). That in itself showed up the Corinthian attitude but Paul rams home the point by showing how that rich generosity was out of extreme poverty.

That is an amazing fact. Most people would think that poverty gave one a clear and fair reason for not giving to others, but not so in Macedonia. No wonder

Paul can speak of their giving as 'the grace that God has given' (v. 1). That sort of giving comes from the heart; and the heart does not sit down to calculate but responds in love when it sees need. 'When I earn wages or a salary then I'll start to give,' says a student but other Christian students have learnt to give already – it is always possible. 'If I earned more I would start giving,' said someone to me – but the heart finds ways to give even in poverty, for it is not so much the amount but the attitude. If – as many do – we start from 'how little can I give' we remain like that. But the Macedonians started from 'how much can I give' and probably surprised even themselves with the results!

Smiling as you give

Well, says Mr. Hang-on-to-what-I've-got, they must have found it very hard to give from their poverty. Not so, says Paul, although they were also in 'severe trial' they gave out of 'overflowing joy' (verse 2). To the non-Christian or the unreleased Christian, that is simply staggering and impossible to believe. Yet joy and giving are inseparably linked. I have had the privilege of being the minister to congregations in Manchester and London that have tackled huge building projects for Christ, requiring considerable financial sacrifice. I can tell you that in both places, as the projects developed, the givers became more joyful and the non-givers or reluctant givers became more miserable. On the major Gift Days, a look across the congregation showed in a flash who gave and who did not! I remember a little old lady, living in a very simple house in Manchester, wondering how she could give. Suddenly she remembered the only valuable thing she possessed – a lovely dinner service tucked away in a box. She went and sold it and brought the proceeds to my house. As she gave it to me her face was radiant and she was crying with joy. Jesus's words really are true in experience: 'It is more blessed to give than to receive' (Acts 20:35). It is a truth that flies in the face of the 'get, get, get' world in which we live.

A tenth for God?

Now Paul speaks, in verse 3, of two standards of giving – that which was 'as much as they were able' and that which was 'beyond their ability'. It is the realm of what seems generous and reasonable moving into the realm of daring and love. Elsewhere in Scripture we have the principle similarly expressed in terms of tithing (a tenth) and offering (e.g. in Malachi 3:8).

Tithes are the proportionate side of giving. Christians who reject the idea of tithing on the grounds that it is Old Testament legalism need to check themselves that their New Testament freedom does not result in a lesser standard of giving! For many of us, the tithing of our income is basic to Christian living. The usual reluctance had to be overcome but anyone who has adopted the tithing principle will say that it has been a new dimension in their giving. It means that God has a first claim on our income and not the remnants of what we can afford when we have spent what we want on ourselves. The practical steps of putting the actual cash on one side each week or month, or of setting up a separate bank account, or of some other helpful method, means that you start by thinking of living on the other nine-tenths. The money for the Lord and for needs in the world is set aside, and regular giving is possible and thought-through. The sharing in the offering at church services becomes not an embarrassing feature but a positive part of our worship.

Some may object to the idea of an actual tenth. If so, then at least think in terms of proportionate giving. If you do not get into that way of thinking, your giving remains static even when your income increases. But if you do get into it then your giving corresponds to earnings or unemployment pay or pension or pocket money or whatever we receive. It is not the actual amount we put on the offertory plate but how it relates to our income. A five-pound note, or ten dollars, may seem a lot for some people but is mingy for others earning high salaries. It is helpful to overhaul our tithing each year at the moment we complete our tax returns and see the total of our income for the past year.

Then start offering!

However, the tithing principle (whether before tax or after tax, whether after rent or mortgage payments or before – that is something for us to work out before God) is only part of the story. The Macedonians gave proportionately ('as they were able') and beyond. The 'beyond' is the realm of 'offerings' – which may be spontaneous and responding to special needs or as a special act of love towards the Lord. We have the woman with the alabaster box and the pouring out of the expensive ointment over Jesus. Those watching regarded it as a waste, but it was an act of love and Jesus received it.

I remember a young man in my youth group years ago who was deeply moved in his heart. He wanted to express the new love he had for God and wanted to do so in an outward and visible way. He went to his bank and drew out his savings and gave them in their entirety for the Lord's work. The next week I had a letter from his father protesting about his son's action and demanding that the money be returned.

The young man did not want to have it returned and so it went into the Lord's work. It was his special love gift – an offering of thanksgiving and love that had sprung from his renewed heart. Little wonder, perhaps, that the same young man later went on to offer his life for the Lord's service and is now in the ordained ministry.

Offerings may be on special Gift Days in our churches, or when there is a special call for relief in a country or for world need in general or for an urgent need in a friend's life or with someone in our fellowship. It may also not be generated by need but, as with the young man I mentioned, by overwhelming love or gratitude – for the birth of a child, the healing of an illness, the answer to a special prayer, the loveliness of a holiday, the blessing of a sermon, a new understanding of God, the passing of exams, the love of a friend, or the memory of a life.

Quite often I have seen an envelope or a roll of notes in the offering plate or through the post with an anonymous note saying 'in great gratitude to God for His blessing. . .'. Here, in verse 3, the offerings that went beyond the scale of proportionate giving flowed because the Macedonians saw need and their hearts wanted to meet it. How little could they have known that their loving act would be an example to Christians for thousands of years!

Please may we give!

The next sentence adds even more lustre to the picture. We are told that they 'pleaded for the privilege' of sharing in this relief of others. Once again, their attitude was the complete opposite of the reluctant givers who try to look the other way when the offering happens or is mentioned! They regarded giving not as a burden but as a privilege. You can only explain that by the grace of God flowing in their hearts.

We hear of the need in another part of the world – perhaps of the church undergoing persecution or of areas of famine and starvation. If we can share by giving we are to see it as a privilege. Doesn't that transform things? It's a long way from 'I suppose I ought to do something about it'. When we place our offering envelope in the Sunday collection, we should see it as a privilege. I look back on the enormous sums of money given for the rebuilding of All Souls – given by ordinary Christians with amazing sacrifice – and I know that all of us involved can say 'it was a privilege to be part of this investment for God', an investment that has paid constant dividends in the lives of thousands in the succeeding years.

And we give ourselves

Cash can be an alternative to close involvement and we must make sure that it is not so. Verse 5 tells us that the Macedonians did not allow it to be 'cold' but gave themselves first to the Lord and then to Paul, and so to the concerns he shared with them. Giving to world need should be matched by a close interest in the facts of that need and of the people in need – an interest overflowing in prayer. When the need is close at hand we can often be personally involved in practical action.

In one parish where I worked there were some terrible houses – and families living in appalling conditions. Practical action took place. People took time off from work and, as teams, tackled houses from top to bottom in cleaning, in replacing beds and bedding, in trying to restore homeliness. Total transformations were achieved in a day – and all was due to the giving of people *as* people, as well as in money to buy the new furniture.

The Macedonians felt a close involvement from afar. They could not 'come alongside' because of the distance, but they could share in love and, no doubt, prayer. Giving has to start with ourselves. It has to spring out of a heart given to God and a life surrendered to Him or else it is a remote 'arm's length' activity.

A proof of love

Such an example must have left the Corinthians breathless with embarrassment – possibly with resentment. Paul continues to press his attack on their selfish defences. Titus (v. 6) was being sent to collect this 'act of grace' on their part. They would have to face him and not send excuses from a distance. Paul urges them (with a lovely piece of added encouragement in his commendation of their faith, knowledge, earnestness and love for him) to 'excel also in this grace of giving'. It was a glaring lack in their Christian experience. They had to start giving as God intended. The reason is deeper than the money released; it is (v. 8) a test of 'the sincerity of their love'.

It is easy to say 'I love God' and even to join in exuberant expressions of love and worship towards God as the Corinthians enjoyed doing. But if, when it comes down to the realistic and practical terms that affect our pocket and possessions, there is no love, the words we utter are empty and hollow.

I have found this always to be true in the giving projects in which I have been involved. The challenge to 'think of the greatest amount you can give and then double it' which Bishop Alf Stanway commended wherever he went, presses us to action; and yet that action can only be out of love. The two work hand in hand, even stimulating each other, so that the spiritual always outmatches the material and people who have learned to give from the heart in love find that they themselves are gloriously blessed in the process with a new experience of the flowing love of our marvellous God. It is therefore a test of the genuineness of our love – a test in which some groups of Christians who exult in God in worship fail miserably.

Jesus the great giver

Love needs constant renewal and there is no greater source of that renewal than in our Lord Jesus. When our love grows weak we are refreshed when we turn to think of Him and of his sacrificial love for us on the Cross. We saw that in chapter 5 when Paul was tackling the Corinthians' reluctance to witness; now we see it here in tackling the reluctance to give. So in verse 9 we have that gem of a verse on the grace of Jesus Christ – setting aside riches to become poor for us, that we might, through his poverty, become rich. He gave all. He left everything. He gave himself utterly. Isn't it a searching twist of the words to speak of our becoming rich through his poverty? It is not the kind of phrase that would spring naturally to our lips. We would more readily speak of being saved, or having forgiveness or eternal life. But, using the context of the chapter, Paul speaks of our becoming rich.

We are reminded of his words in 1 Corinthians 3:21 'All things are yours . . . and you are Christ's and Christ is God's' (RSV). How much is opened up to us, both now and in eternity, when we are 'in Christ'. All of it is only possible because Jesus gave to the uttermost. 'Love so amazing, so divine, demands my life, my soul, my all.'

Put your money where your mouth is

Paul returns to some practical pressure (v. 10ff). Apparently when Paul first asked the churches to give for this relief project, the Corinthians started doing so but they did not carry it through. Their enthusiasm or commitment did not go on to completion. Regrettably, that is a frequent trait in church circles. The division between commitment and casualness is sharp. The committed person will carry through their task or their responsibility with unswerving loyalty to Christ. The casual person will not have the same sense of commitment to the task because, it seems, he does not have the same commitment to Christ. He does not see that he is letting Christ down – only ('only'!!) the church or other people. The task lapses. The promise to give fades away. Paul challenges the Corinthians to take up the task and to complete what 'a year ago' they had promised. He assures them in verse 12 that they are not expected to give what they do not have (presumably they had put that up as an excuse) nor so to give that others are relieved while they are in difficulty (v. 13) but that he is aiming at an equality that shares with those in need and receives from those who are in a better state of provision. This is the communal aspect of Christianity working out between churches, as part of the body of Christ.

The collectors are coming!

If the Corinthians had by this time braced themselves for Titus coming to collect, they now had to brace themselves for a bigger shock. From 8:16 to 9:5 he lets them know that Titus will be accompanied by a brother who has been praised by all the churches for his service to the gospel, and another 'zealous' brother who has 'great confidence' in the Corinthians. How-

ever, this is only the advance party! They are being
sent (9.5) to prepare the arrangements for receiving
the 'generous gift' the Corinthians had promised. So
who was to come when it was prepared? The Corinthians pride is about to be dented even further . . .
for Paul suggests bringing Macedonians with him
(v. 4). That really was salt in the wound! It is one
thing to have another church set up as an example
but when their representatives come to spur us to be
like them it is humiliating! The 'with me' of verse 4
shelters under the blow of the announcement regarding the Macedonians. Yes, Paul is coming himself!

Batter those defences

Now, do you see how Paul puts on the pressure? It
is one thing piled on another, blow after blow comes
to bring about the 'knock-out'. The only explanation
of this is that giving does not happen easily or readily;
if a person is to become a giver as God intends then
the brass gates of his defences have to be shattered.
It often takes a series of challenges, expositions, sermons, straight talking and demonstrations of need,
for the gates to fall. When they do fall, they fall for
ever and an enormous amount of giving in time,
money and service is released for the kingdom of
Christ. This part of 2 Corinthians is a charter to
hammer away about giving in spite of the squeals of
protest it will generate. We have biblical warrant.
Paul aims at total surrender by the Corinthians on
this issue and the release of love in giving.

Responsible distribution

It is important to note that Paul takes a special care
to be honest and beyond criticism about the handling
of money for God. Look back to chapter 8 verses 20–

21. We need to be acting rightly in the eyes of men as well as the eyes of God. This means great care in the counting and handling of offerings in churches or collections at meetings or in any monies given for the relief of need or the service of Christ. Money that is uncounted should never be handled alone; there should be independent checks. No one should be trusted to act on his own – for his sake and for the sake of the church.

An incident where a trusted member of the church was discovered to have salted away hundreds and hundreds of pounds under the noses of other counters present at the table, which occurred a few years ago in a church I know, was extremely painful to everyone. Yet, more than that, it dishonoured Christ. Sometimes I go to a Christian meeting and am handed cash for the travelling. No receipt is requested and so what check is there on the honesty of the treasurer? He will normally be strictly honest but he also needs to be *seen* to be honest – 'in the eyes of men' (8.21). Correct procedures are part of our responsibility for God.

I have known Christian ministers and leaders who have not heeded this example from Scripture. There was no suggestion of their being dishonest but because they did not keep proper accounts and so could not answer the critics who wanted them 'to give an account of their stewardship', suspicion, pain and strained fellowship resulted.

You reap what you sow

The truth of sowing and reaping in the natural world is here applied in the sphere of giving. It is not, of course, a straight sowing of cash and a harvest of cash as some persuasive cults want us to believe. 'Send twenty pounds or forty dollars and within six months you will have ten times the amount back from God' (such statements are always accompanied by numerous examples of Mr. X at such and such a place and Miss Y elsewhere who are now rich because they gave to this guru, prophet or organization). It is a despicable misapplication of the reaping picture in the Bible and puts the Christian faith into hard cash-investment terms, resulting in our own material benefit.

The New Testament does not rule out material blessings, as we shall see further on in this chapter, but does not speak in such materialistic terms as the give-and-get philosophy offers. Rather, the harvest is in richer spiritual terms. Tens of thousands could testify genuinely to that. Giving does bring spiritual blessing – as long as it is giving from the heart.

In the Old Testament, God says he despises the gifts brought because the people's hearts are so far from him. So here Paul links the sowing reaping quotation (which is similarly expressed in Proverbs 11:24: 'One man gives freely, yet grows all the richer – another withholds what he should give and suffers want') with the attitude. God, he says in 9:7, loves a cheerful giver. He does not want gifts that are given out of a sense of duty or obligation or because the giver cannot avoid the persuasive techniques of the fund-raisers. He does not want reluctant giving but cheerful giving. Take this seriously. I have said, on the basis of this text, at many Gift Days when we have had colossal targets for our giving: 'Don't give unless you do so in love for Christ . . . If you feel you ought to give but your heart is not in it, please do not give anything at all . . . we only want giving that springs from love for the Lord.' The key to all giving is in the heart.

I attend meetings sometimes where fund-raising for Christian purposes is on the agenda. The means and methods suggested are the same as for a non-Christian cause. They are persuasion and manipulation. They look to see if there are many rich people whom they could approach. It is all on the wrong track. Giving comes from the heart, not from the wallet. Rich people often cannot give because they are too tied up with possessions (although I hasten to say that some rich people give marvellously and go on and on giving) and yet often the ordinary person can really give. The heart is the key, so prayer is vital in a giving project. Here in 9:7 God, who looks on the heart, tells us that only cheerful giving is acceptable. Smile as you give – because you give in love!

God is no man's debtor

Yet there is an assurance of God's provision for us when we give. The closed-fist philosophy brings little blessing, if any, as Scrooge discovered. The open-handed approach means that God can meet us with his blessing (Malachi 3 again – we are promised blessings more than we can contain when we stop robbing God and bring the full tithes into the storehouse). He is able (v. 8) to make all grace abound towards us. So the grace of giving in us is matched by fresh grace from Him. The results will be in having enough to meet our needs (not our luxuries) and in enabling us to be more fruitful servants of his in the world. The talents parable of Jesus teaches us that the reward of good service is further responsibility! So here the reward of giving is in terms partly of 'good work' for Him. The physical and spiritual are again matched in verse 10. Not only will we have an adequate store of seed (needs met) but a greater 'harvest of righteousness'.

The person who spends everything on himself – on records, books, films, entertainment, magazines, expensive holidays, luxuries – never finds satisfaction.

He finds a fleeting sense of satisfaction but not in terms that last and get deeper as the years go by. The giver finds that true satisfaction, and finds it deepening. There is a glorious reward within one's own spirit and this is part of the 'harvest of righteousness' within us.

Another part of that harvest comes from a rightness before God over material things which blesses our spirit and helps us to have a truer perspective on life. The 'rich' reference in verse 11 must mean in the spirit as well as in an attitude to possessions. The progression seems to be: We experience God's love and grace in Jesus; we respond in love and grace to others; God responds in more love and grace to us; we respond in further love and grace to others. It is an increasing experience so that the true giver becomes more and more a generous person sharing himself and his possessions with others.

So the Corinthians are being encouraged to think in these God-intended terms. If they say 'we can't afford to give to this relief fund' they will not find God's promised blessing and will shrivel within their spirits. But if they say 'we can't afford it but we are going to share in any case', they will find that God actually enables them to give, that he makes up what is given and more, and that then they will be able to give more, and then know further blessing . . . and so on. I can testify to the truth of this in many lives as well as in our own family. People who have dared to give beyond any reasonable calculation have found God matching and supplying – a tax rebate, a gift, a rise in wages or salary – making up what has been given and yet often richly so. The darers over giving keep being surprised. The reluctant and mingy have no such surprises. Their giving (if it can be called that) has predictable results.

The by-product of thanksgiving

There is a lovely by-product to real giving. It is the by-product of thanksgiving (see the end of chapter 9 verse 11 and then verse 12). It is an important 'also'. Paul envisages in his mind's eye the recipients of the relief gifts he is wanting out of the Corinthians, fellow-believers in impoverished circumstances being materially helped and spiritually uplifted to thanksgiving. Our minds can go across the world to refugee camps, to beleagured churches in countries ruled by atheistic governments or dictators, to those caught in a great drought or a failure of local harvest, or to those in countries where lawlessness has meant no crops and little hope. The arm of Christians can reach out in love not only in prayer but in the basic material terms of cash.

In 1982 the Polish crisis brought forth thousands and thousands of pounds from Christians to buy food and supplies for the churches to handle and distribute in that country. One could imagine the churches meeting and receiving the lorry and its supplies for them. There would be joy and relief – but there would also be great thanksgiving to God for His mercy through his people. They will praise God, says Paul in verse 13, not just because of the relief but because it demonstrates the outworking of the gospel of Christ in the lives of the senders.

The social gospel, so-called, and the Christian gospel are not rivals. The gospel of salvation in Jesus is the greatest need of the world – but the accompaniment of practical love and relief where it is needed should serve to glorify Christ and show the truth of the gospel.

Paul so many times in this letter points out the 'knock-on effects' (as with comfort in chapter one). Here he sees that the recipients will give thanks to

God and then will start praying for the givers. They will be drawn to the givers by the grace shown in the giving and new bonds of love will be accompanied by fresh blessing in answer to prayer. Paul stops there but we could continue the circle. Fresh blessing will surely result in fresh action and so the wheel goes full circle.

The final sentence of these dynamic chapters points us back to the inspiration of all giving: to Jesus, to the free gift of salvation offered to all who believe, to the greatest gift offered to man. Our response must be one of exultant thanksgiving – in our life on earth, in the way we live and give and share, and then with the gathered company of God's people in heaven. Now, and then, we exclaim, 'Thanks be to God for his indescribable gift!'

8: War and captivity
10:1–11:13

It's war!

'Don't you know there's a war on?' That was a common remark in the Second World War. It ought to be common amongst Christians. The picture of sweetness and comfort that many want Christianity to be is a long way from the spiritual battleground revealed to us in Jesus's life and throughout the New Testament. 'Our struggle is not against flesh and blood' says Paul in Ephesians 6, 'but against the rulers, against authorities, against the powers of this dark world and against the spiritual forces of evil in the heavenly realms.' In this part of 2 Corinthians, Paul opens up to us the warfare being waged against the church, often from within. Satan is shown as aiming to divert Christians from the truth in Jesus and to replace the true faith with false substitutes. The Corinthians had become an easy prey to Satanic attack and we need to weigh the warnings of this passage deeply in our hearts. They are of urgent relevance to the church of today.

Into battle!

Firstly, Paul calls us to battle ourselves. It is not just a matter of defence against Satan but attack upon him by the church. We are (v. 3) to 'wage war'. How? Not as the world does. There is no place at all for Christianity to be forced on people at the point of a sword or gun or by offer of material aid. This has often been the way of heresies and, tragically and to our shame, sometimes of the Christian church; but it has no place in God's plan. The church has to be careful about using clever techniques or slick methodology such as bringing the gospel to people with the persuasive methods of an encyclopaedia salesman. If a person is forced into the kingdom by the church then the church will have to stand guard on him for all time; whereas when the Holy Spirit draws someone He will stand guard for eternity. So (v. 4) 'the weapons we fight with are not the weapons of the world'. We are in a spiritual battle – a battle for the eternal destiny of men and women, a battle for the truth of God, a battle for the spiritual state of human beings.

This battle can only be won by spiritual weapons. Just as we cannot stop a bullet with a plastic raincoat, or stop a radio wave with a fly-swat or stop germ warfare with a gun, so we cannot stop Satanic warfare by methods and gimmicks and organization. It can only be done by the word of God and prayer.

It is the same in the witness we make to the truth of the gospel. What will reach through to the inner man is the word – for the 'word of God is living and active. Sharper than any double-edged sword, it penetrates even to dividing soul and spirit, joints and marrow; it judges the thoughts and attitudes of the heart' (Hebrews 4:12). All evangelism, witness and contesting for the truth of God must concentrate on handling that sword effectively – in communication and explanation and proclamation. At the same time we need to be men and women who surround the work of witness with prayer. So often prayer gatherings in churches are merely concerned with domestic and personal needs and do not begin to see the vital necessity of supporting the preaching, the evangelizing and all the outgoing work of the church with fervent prayer. Things happen in a church and in a neighbourhood when the Christians really pray. We are waging war and we are complete fools to think we can succeed by any other means than by the weapons of the word and prayer.

Watch it come down!

The spiritual weapons are powerful (vs. 4–5). They can demolish strongholds. Isn't that an enormous encouragement? You may perhaps be a Christian in a difficult situation – perhaps finding yourself ridiculed in your college by a lecturer or professor who repeatedly uses you as a butt of his humour and tries to make you look ignorant simply because you are a Christian. Look again at the text. The stronghold of that man's philosophy has no protection against spiritual weapons. The reason, of course, is that atheistic philosophies are on a false foundation and when they are really attacked they find their 'foundations' crumbling.

Many Christians today have learnt how to get inside the non-Christian philosophies so that they can expose the weakness of them and press the holder of such a philosophy to the logical conclusions of his position. At the same time the effective witnesser is to show the eternal foundations of the faith in Christ. During the first Festival of Light Rally in London, when tens of thousands of Christians assembled to march to Hyde Park, many atheists went to the Park to vilify the Christians. One such man, a person of high intellect holding down an important job, went to attack the Christians. He was shaken by the force of the atheistic attack and the vile things being said; but he was more shaken by the love of the Christians in response. A crack appeared in his atheistic armour! He began to search and came to our church 'by accident' when we had a big evangelistic service. His defences crumbled. He turned to Christ. Suddenly his intellect was geared to the new life he had found. He read several books a week and grew rapidly as a powerful advocate for Jesus. His stronghold – which had appeared so impregnable – had been destroyed by love and the word and prayer.

The deeply moving account of C. S. Lewis's coming out of his atheism into Christ is a constant encouragement to recall. The cracks in his position as an atheist gradually appeared and he found himself steadily exposed by the truth of God. He was, at first, the 'most reluctant convert'! But his stronghold crumbled before the word of God. So let us take courage when we face people who seem impregnable in their stance against God. No-one is impregnable against the word and prayer. Begin to pray for your enemies, for those who mock you and try to humiliate you intellectually, – pray for the destroying of their strongholds and, when opportunity arises, handle the sword of the word that it may break through every remaining defence!

Into captivity – for Christ

We aim at a captivity to Christ (v. 5). At first sight that seems to give credence to the false charge that you have to surrender intellectual integrity if you become a Christian. From the outside it may appear like that but all of us who have come to Christ know that the opposite is true. We would want to say (wouldn't we?) that the fear of the Lord really is the beginning of wisdom and that our whole way of thinking became transformed.

How is this possible? It is only possible because a person who surrenders to Jesus Christ as Saviour and Lord receives the Holy Spirit. The Holy Spirit searches and knows the things of God and shows them to us (1 Cor. 2). We suddenly find the Bible lighting up to us and we begin to see, as never before, how utterly relevant God's truth is to the world in which we live. God's analysis of man is the only one that makes sense. God's way of living; God's way of human beings being right with him; God's values of life, justice and so on. We now think in terms of this being *God's* world; everything fits into that frame and makes sense. We now see ourselves as created in the image of God – a little lower than the angels and not just a little higher than the animals. The totality of our thinking changes.

So when we hear Paul speaking here of bringing every thought into captivity – into obedience to Christ – we are speaking about freedom, in place of the captivity and bondage in which man stands before he turns to Christ. We are speaking of being in Christ who is the way, the truth and the life.

Under authority

Not only is this passage about the witness of Christians but about the on-going life in Christ. There is always a double picture in the New Testament: the victory of Christ in which we share eternally when we turn to him, and the 'mopping up' operations that go on for life. We are dead in Christ and alive in Christ – that is our eternal state. But much needs to be 'put off' and 'put on' as Ephesians 4 and Colossians 3 spell out so frankly and helpfully. It is not, as some teach, that because we are dead and risen we have nothing more to do about practical holiness. Rather, because we are dead and risen we should live out what we are.

We should wage war on the tangles of sin and the infection of evil as well as fostering all that belongs to the Spirit of God in love, fruitfulness and goodness. So the plea here in verses 5 and 6 is to the Corinthians to get on with submission to the truth of God and to stop disobeying what God has revealed to them in Christ.

The Corinthians were all for a happy effervescent worship gathering as often as possible but not for a close attention to the word of God and to living in obedience to the revealed truth of God. Paul sees it as his responsibility to exercise discipline and to 'punish disobedience'. There cannot be a free-for-all, an 'every man doing what he thinks is right'; there must be a growing concern to live as Christ wants us to live. The discipline intended is not authoritarian – the leader telling people what to do and what not to do. This sort of discipling-legalism has flourished from time to time and is particularly common in some small groups of Christians today. Instead it is a matter of the authority of the word and helping people to submit to that. The leader or teacher only has authority as he handles the authoritative word and leads in the light of it.

Many Christians resent any correction. If there is a gentle exposure of a fault, a covetous attitude, a temper, a lack of love, a hypocritical approach – the exposed person resents it and leaves the church. God grants that you and I will always bring criticism or correction of our lives to the bar of Scripture and, where that correction is valid, repent and submit ourselves afresh to the glad captivity of Christ. This is Paul's aim here. Those who resisted and rejected what he was saying would have to face discipline by him. In those days they could not go off to another church in Corinth!

Beyond comparison?

Smug self-confidence can be the most difficult barrier of all to Christian reality. At least when a Christian meets an atheist or an agnostic both sides know clearly where they stand. But the person who thinks he is all right and a perfectly good Christian ('better than the lot who go to church' and so on) has to be shown what he is really like before God and not what he thinks he is like. Verses 7–18 have such people in mind. They only look 'on the surface of things'. The smooth-speaking and attractive false apostles in Corinth had mesmerised the church. They seemed great people – not a bit like Paul whose appearance was apparently not very attractive. Now they had committed themselves to those false apostles they felt they were right and Paul was wrong. Indeed, they seemed almost to go as far as doubting whether Paul was a genuine Christian. He had not 'arrived' like them – he was still not at their supposed higher spiritual level. Some of us have to put up with the same treatment today; it is such a strength to know it happened to Paul too! So Paul says, in effect, (v. 7) 'At least regard us as fellow-Christians!' Then he takes it further. He deftly begins to expose their thinking (v. 12ff). What they are doing is comparing themselves with themselves! They look at the false apostles in their midst and are content if they have the same level of Christian living – possibly the same 'badges' of particular gifts or actions or ways in worship. There is an inbuilt security which Paul here seeks to dynamite. For that is not captivity to the obedience of Christ but captivity to the obedience of men. The Christian must see that there is only one possible comparison to be made that is valid – and that is measuring ourselves by Christ Jesus Himself.

Who is Lord?

Paul had every justification to write strongly to the Corinthians. He was their spiritual father. They had been part of the harvest field assigned to him by the Lord and so that was where he had come. As a spiritual father to them he has a continuing concern and care. He wants to see his 'children in the faith' growing, and verse 15 suggests that the Corinthians were trying to stop his activity amongst them and influence upon them. Paul does not let go so easily. At the same time, he does not want to be so caught up sorting out the Corinthians that he is prevented from 'preaching the gospel in regions beyond' (v. 16). Paul has the burning heart of an evangelist and is always looking outward for the fresh opportunities to exercise that mission.

There is plenty that Paul could boast about as he looks back to his mission to Corinth but just when his readers might think that was what he was doing he turns the argument back into true perspective. If we are going to boast at all, let us 'boast in the Lord'. For it is His work and not ours. If we want commendation, let us not seek it by self-congratulation and smug self-satisfaction, but rather at the feet of Christ. So, again, Paul presses the point of this chapter – for it follows that if we do not bring every thought into obedience to Christ we cannot expect Christ's commendation. This is a vital key to all of our living and our ministry – Christ must always be at the centre and everything we do must be brought to his feet. In everything – everything – Christ must be pre-eminent.

The third party

The letter now becomes even more serious. The warfare waged by Satan has had shattering effects upon the Corinthians in the arena of truth. Those who uphold the Corinthian church as the model for Christian worship and church life seem never to realise that Corinth went into heresy. When experience matters most, truth suffers.

Biblical truth and spiritual experience go hand in hand and must never be divorced. Truth without experience is deadly; experience without truth is disastrous. Corinth is an example of such disaster. Chapter 11 verses 1–5 is a 'church's health warning'. The passion of Paul's heart bursts into anguish. He had brought them to Christ, like the friend of the bridegroom. The church is the bride of Christ and Paul, in Ephesians 5, tells us how the Lord Jesus longs for the bride to be without spot, or wrinkle or any blemish. This is what Paul longed for the Corinthian church to be. He wanted them to have eyes for Jesus only, as a bride to her bridegroom. This is Paul's own longing – to be found in Christ, to grow in Christ, to be more like Christ. Now he had to look on while a 'third party' diverted the Corinthians from Christ. There is no doubt in Paul's mind as to who is behind the false apostles who have done this – it is Satan. Nor is there any doubt that Satan's tactics are always those of trying to divert from the Lord as he did in deceiving Eve.

Satan in at the top

Look on to verse 13–15 for a moment. See there the devastating description of those false apostles. Read it as a Corinthian might have done, with his own viewpoint that these men were in fact marvellous messengers of God and super-spiritual apostles. Paul's words must have stung and probably angered them. Those apostles are 'false apostles, deceitful workmen, masquerading as apostles of Christ'. Strong words.

There would be howls of opposition if we used such terms of such people today, for we have often been sweet and soft towards heresy and so let it flourish. Now Paul presses the point harder still. These apostles are not just false – they are Satanic. They are Satan's servants masquerading as servants of righteousness. What better tactic can an enemy have than to infiltrate the very ranks and leadership of his enemy and even to command? If Satan could infiltrate the leadership of the Christian church at local or national or international level, would he not do it? And has he not done it? This is not a charter for a witch-hunt. No such hunt is necessary. The test is always that of obedience to Christ and his word. Where leadership swerves from that it is either on the slippery slope to error or has already been infiltrated by the enemy. We must never think that we can test by any test except Christ – whatever the 'rank' of the Christian leader.

Turned from Christ

So what had happened? Go back to verses 3–6. The Corinthians had been diverted from their 'sincere and pure devotion to Christ'. This diverting had been by persuasive preachers. To the Corinthians the untrained speaking abilities of Paul (v. 6) seemed totally outclassed by those smooth-tongued 'apostles'. Paul realises that they appeared to the Corinthian eyes as 'super-apostles' (v. 5). Yet it is content that matters and not eloquence or oratory. The tests are: is it true? is it in accordance with God's word? is it lifting up the true Jesus? So Paul says that (v. 6) 'I may not be a trained speaker, but I do have knowledge'. That is what matters and because the Corinthians could not discern that they fell into at least three major heretical errors, spelt out in verse 4.

Another Jesus

The first error was to turn to 'another Jesus'. The Greek here means a 'different kind' of Jesus, not a different Jesus. Did they make Jesus more God than man, more man than God – or what? We do not know. But we do know that down through the centuries and in the present day we have that sort of error. There are those who want to present Jesus as man only – a good man, a teacher, someone to be followed and admired, but not God. Some say he was not born of the Holy Spirit, others that he had no existence prior to his birth by Mary. There are those who speak of Jesus as the human man and Christ as the divine idea; others who deny the divinity of Jesus and say that only a likeness died on the Cross; and yet others who so minimize the human side of Jesus that it seems almost not to matter whether he walked this earth and died for us, as long as you can have a mystical experience of his resurrection life today. It is all so far from the simplicity and clarity of the true Jesus Christ revealed to us in the New Testament – truly God and truly man. Never let yourself be led astray from that sincere and pure devotion to Christ that is central to a living Christian faith; test the theories of theologians by the one test God has given us – Scripture.

A different spirit

The second error was to receive 'a different spirit'. The Greek here means a different spirit altogether – not a different kind of spirit. This is alarming. It means that these Christians in Corinth – so proud of their spiritual experiences – were in fact not indwelt by the Holy Spirit. What they were exhibiting was a pseudo-spirituality. This is a serious charge.

John sustains a similar charge in his first letter, chapter 4. It is deeply disturbing. Test the spirits, he says. 'This is how you can recognize the spirit of God: Every spirit that acknowledges that Jesus Christ has come in the flesh is from God, but every spirit that does not acknowledge Jesus is not from God.' Then comes this sentence: 'This is the spirit of antichrist.' Is that what was happening in Corinth? Was the apparent spirituality actually a spirit of anti-Christ, rotting away spiritual foundations from within? It seems in the New Testament that we can interpret the concept of a completely different spirit in no other way. If it is not the Holy Spirit it must be the counterfeit and deceiving spirit of anti-Christ.

The New Testament encourages us to look for the fruit as the test also. Jesus is uncompromising in his Sermon on the Mount. There, in Matthew 7:15–23 we are told to test all prophets by their fruit: 'By their fruit you will recognize them.' There would be those who would put their trust in their special works, in prophesying, driving out demons and in performing miracles. No doubt, like some today, they regarded these as marks of special spiritual grace. But Jesus decimates them. When they come to him, calling him Lord, and bringing evidence of their works, he will reply 'I never knew you.' This does not make prophesying, miracles and so on wrong. However, it does make them wrong as a means of assurance. Fruit – love, joy, peace, holiness of life – this is God's test. This fruit seemed to have little place in the Corinthian thinking. So Paul has to major on the importance and priority of love (1 Corinthians 13) in the middle of chapters on gifts. The true Spirit of God will be bringing forth his fruit – the character of Jesus – in the believer. The counterfeit spirit – the anti-Christ – will be evidenced by 'pushiness', self-concern, spiritual pride and superiority, over-attention to the occult and spirit-activities, and carelessness with the truth.

A different gospel

The third error was in their acceptance of a 'different gospel'. Again, the Greek means a different gospel altogether – not a different version of the gospel. Galatians 1:6–9 is a blistering attack on the acceptance of 'another gospel' which, says Paul, is 'no gospel at all'. He continues in those searing words: 'Even if we or an angel from heaven should preach a gospel other than the one we preached to you, let him be eternally condemned!' There is no hint of the idea, prevalent even today, that salvation can be by other means than the grace of God in Jesus Christ and his sacrifice for our sins on the Cross. As no other gospel can save men, there is utmost importance in fighting for the one true gospel. Justification is by faith through grace. We receive salvation as a gift from God. We can never earn it. Anything that subtracts from this gospel or adds to it things necessary for salvation, is not the gospel. So often, the alternative offered seems more attractive, easier to accept, less demanding, more inclusive, and so, like the Corinthians, many turn to it 'easily enough' (v. 4).

In the centre of the ring

Paul's passion cascades over the Corinthians whom he loves deeply in spite of their foolishness. He wants to cut the ground from under those who have tried to make themselves apostles equal to him. He is out in the centre of the ring fighting: fighting for the truth, fighting for the souls of men and women. He knows that, as far as the false teachers are concerned, 'their end will be what their actions deserve' (v. 15) – and we may say the same today as we groan over false teachers and false theologians – but he does not want the end of these his 'children in the faith' in Corinth to be the same. He is therefore in an all-out rescue bid to restore them to a sincere and pure devotion to Christ. May God give us such passion too that we may not only be concerned to proclaim Christ but to rescue those going astray from the faith. We are in a spiritual war – a quiet opting-out is not an option for a Christian. Our aim must always be to 'take captive every thought to make it obedient to Christ'.

9: Power, grace and testing
11:16–13:14

Suffering for Christ

Suffering did not have much place in the teaching of
the superlative apostles in Corinth. We saw this in the
earlier chapters but the theme now bursts out again.
Paul is goaded by the boastings of those teachers to
do some boasting himself. He hastens to tell us, in
verse 17, that his boasting is not what the Lord would
do but that he feels it is the only way to reply to those
Corinthian misleaders. Their marks of superiority
were in terms of attractive speaking and an apparent
freedom from trouble. Paul's are the opposite – the
power of God manifested in him in spite of not being
a trained speaker and the power of God shown in his
sufferings for Christ.

Loss of discernment

Paul is further goaded into this outburst because of
the naivety of the Corinthians (verses 19–21). It is
every bit as true today that when Christians divert to
a by-path, to a super-spiritual segment or to any de-
flection from the centrality of Christ, they seem to
lose discernment. They cease to see anything wrong
in the group-thinking to which they have turned (and
they see little if anything right with anyone else!).

When some of us ache about such treatment we can take comfort that Paul felt the same. The Corinthians thought themselves wise (v. 19) and were so under the spell of the false teachers that they would submit to being enslaved, exploited and taken advantage of or pushed around. The sharpest and most distressing evidences of this have been in the terrible results of heretical movements centred round some person – such as the one resulting in the Jonestown massacre in Guyana. People in such groupings lose all sense; they surrender goods, houses and all their money; they put themselves totally under the whim and will of the leader. Diversions from the centrality of Jesus that do not turn so far to heresy have the same marks in some measure as Paul discerns here in verse 20.

Ready for anything

So Paul boasts. He had the same Jewish ancestry and is equally a servant of Christ. There the comparison ceases. Instead of a comfortable, self-indulgent Christianity that turned inward on itself he was out in the world of his day with courage and daring and vision that still leaves us breathless 2,000 years afterwards. What Paul achieved for Christ in the days of slow travel and little communication is staggering. He tells us that this involved physical costs – imprisonment, flogging, exposure, thirty-nine lashes (five times), beating, stoning, shipwreck and all sorts of dangers on the land. The Jews hated him; the Gentiles hated him. False believers were a danger too – he always had to exercise discernment and learnt not to judge by outward appearances or commendations. Loss of sleep, long hours of work, hunger, thirst, cold – all had been in his experience. And on top of all that he writes 'I face daily the pressure of my concern for all the churches.' I understand the last sentence very well from my own experience.

This great list of the sufferings he endured would not need to have been written if Paul had not been in the glad service of his Master. He would have been safe back in his Jewish enclave, teaching the law. He certainly would not have been let down a city wall in a basket (v. 33)! Paul is urging the Corinthians not to go on despising this list of his experiences with the false spiritual idea that such things shouldn't befall a victorious Christian. They are rather to see that this list is his track record of committed service for his Lord – not to earn salvation – but to live out his membership in the body of Christ and his call as a true apostle for Jesus Christ.

Take up the cross

How much could be added to Paul's list in the record of Christian service over nearly two thousand years! The amazing courage of early witnesses and mission-aries pioneering into deadly areas of the world. The roll of martyrs for the gospel of Jesus is a long and honourable one. When the gospel frees a heart there is no holding what may happen. We are certainly not to 'play it safe' but to have the courage to take up the cross and to follow Christ whatever the cost.

Paul's commitment and wonderful record of com-mitted missionary service has been an inspiration and challenge to Christians ever since. It makes the in-turned self-indulgent happy-happy Christianity of the Corinthians look sick – and so it was.

Experience of glory

Now Paul presses home on the special-experience front. Apparently the false apostles had told great

accounts of their special visions and their hot-line to
God. 'God has told me this . . .' – a statement that
brooks no disagreement! 'This is the prophecy God
has given me . . . this is what God has told me . . .
I have a vision . . . this is what you must do.' It
happens, sadly, today; many Christians fail to use any
discernment but submit meekly to what they feel must
be very spiritual indeed. They feel that the receivers
of this 'hot-line' information must be very special
people.

Hence Paul was regarded as somewhat second-class
in comparison, with his emphasis on truth and Christian living. So he comes back at the Corinthians. If
they want to think in those terms then he can share
his own seventh-heaven experience. Clearly the 'man
in Christ' in verse 2 of chapter 12 is himself. It was
obviously a deep and overwhelming experience that
carried him beyond himself – a manifestation of the
power and love of God – almost a transfiguration
experience. I know a little of that and remember the
overwhelming manifestation of the love and light of
Christ when I knelt in my room, overwhelmed by
God's call to the ministry, and said 'Lord, here am I;
send me.' It was a taste of glory. There have been
other times when the Lord has overwhelmed me with
his presence and love. These are wonderful times. But
they are not the bread and butter of Christian experience. They are the special tokens of love as a foretaste
of heaven. The false apostles may boast in those terms
but they are wrong to do so, says Paul: 'I will not
boast . . . except about my weaknesses.' While we
may rejoice and wonder at the glory experiences of
Jesus in his Transfiguration we know that the greater
glory of Jesus was in his Cross. There in the darkness
of Calvary, with the darkened sky and the bereft soul
crying 'My God, my God' we see the glory; before it
in the Garden of Gethsemane with sweat as drops of

blood we see the glory; and before that as he touches the leper and loves the sinner we see the glory. 'Now is the Son of Man glorified and God is glorified in him' refers to the cross and the atonement (John 13.31). No wonder then that although we may have special tastes of glory to come, the pathway for the followers of Jesus usually means glory through suffering.

Healing for all?

There are many today who deny the place of suffering in the Christian's life. They sincerely believe that if the kingdom came with Jesus it must mean wholeness of body as well as of soul. Those who believe this often bring much healing and comfort but also leave a trail of despondent wrecks along the way. It is part of their teaching to deny that the verses ahead of us now – verses 7–10, have anything to do with physical suffering. They have to take that line to protect their idea but they are wrong. These verses are some of the most precious in the Bible. They teach us a theology of healing and a theology of suffering – for the truth of the Bible is not an 'either or' but a 'both and' in this matter.

A theology of healing

First, in verse 8, there is the theology of healing. 'Three times I pleaded with the Lord to take it away.' The problem was a 'thorn in the flesh' (v. 7). Those who want to avoid this being a physical affliction suggest it was some sin in his life but if that was so it would need repentance. 'Flesh' is flesh – the physical body – and the thorn suggests something that happened to Paul rather than something brought on by himself.

It may be his worsening eyesight to which he refers. Anyway, he tackles it head on with deliberate prayer. The 'three times' indicates special times of prayer, perhaps separated by weeks rather than days. Perhaps he called together his friends to pray or asked others to lay on hands. We need to learn the deliberate purposefulness of his example to us. Healing prayer is too easily just an item amongst many items but it needs special treatment by Christians. Perhaps this will mean a group coming together for an evening of prayer and laying on of hands (as has been my practice in fellowship groups and in the church's praying fellowship), sometimes a special gathering of close Christian friends. Then we need to meet again and again . . . and again. There is no intention by Paul to impose a three-times limit. Often during those prayer times or as a result of them there is deliverance or healing and we are overjoyed at the result of prayer to our loving Father. Then there are those times when gradually the conviction grows that healing is not going to be the pathway of God's glory for us or for the person we are praying for in the group. To flog on and on even to the day of death, as some have done, is to lose the glory-route. So much of what could happen for the glory of Christ is lost. Instead, as we test the conviction before God, we must begin to alter our prayer as Paul did. He does not just turn to putting up with sufferings but goes to the point of boasting in them (v. 9) and delighting in them! Alongside his theology of healing he has a theology of suffering – that this can be a means of glory to Christ. There is no tension if you hold both and progress as Paul shows us here.

But didn't Christ 'carry our sicknesses'?

Now someone may comment that in Matthew 8.17 it says that Christ has carried our sicknesses and that therefore the Christian may believe that on the cross Christ died for our sins and our sicknesses thus bringing wholeness to the believer. Setting aside the query as to whether it can be applied in that way to the cross (for it seems to be applied more to the healing ministry before the cross) it is more important for us to know that the word for sicknesses in Matthew 8.17 is *asthenia*; here in 2 Cor. 12 v. 9 the word translated 'weaknesses' is *asthenia*; and the word translated 'weaknesses' in verse 10 is also *asthenia*. This totally destroys the case built on Matthew 8.17 by some today – as, I guess, it was meant to destroy the same case amongst the superlative apostles in Corinth in Paul's day. If wholeness is the Christian's right, Paul could hardly rejoice in his weaknesses.

There is nothing to be ashamed of if an illness persists and you are not healed. If you have prayed deliberately on several occasions and have begun to sense the Spirit's response that instead this is to be a pathway of suffering for you, then you do not have to see whether you have sinned or lack enough faith. You can begin to glory in your weakness – for Christ's sake.

Think for a moment. Who are the greatest Christians you have ever known? In most cases you will answer, as I will, that the greatest have been those who have triumphed in the midst of suffering, who, like 'Joni', have lived a life more abundant even though they are disabled or ill or suffer in some way.

Grace and glory

There is more to see! If such a triumphing in our weaknesses was by our own strength – by our resolve to glorify Jesus – that would be good in itself; but we do not have to do it alone. The glorious truth is enshrined in verse 8, the Lord's personal assurance to Paul: 'My grace is sufficient for you, for my power is made perfect in weakness.' Once we accept this as His pathway we will begin to know depths of grace we never knew before and will be carried forward with a strength that is not our own.

I think of all those I have known who have walked in this path and have brought glory to God. I pray that if I am called to walk it too I may as truly accept it for his glory. What memories flood the mind of triumph and grace! I think of an elderly Salvation Army officer with whom I had the privilege of staying during a mission at a local church when I was a student. He was wracked with asthma and confined to his bed. Yet, the moment we returned from the meetings he wanted to know what had happened, for he had been praying with all his heart. He would be thrilled with reports of blessing and concerned with reports of opposition or problem. His face radiated with the glow of Jesus and you felt you were in the presence of the Lord in that bedroom sharing with that dear man who turned illness into glory.

Triumph and power

So Paul is able to turn his thorn into triumph. With it, he is able to take (v. 10) insults, hardships, persecutions, difficulties and so to learn a whole new dimension of Christian living – that 'when I am weak, then I am strong'.

Of course, we know it to be true. Strength comes when we are thrown back upon the grace and strength of the Lord Jesus. When we are fit and well, we can be tempted to rely on our own strength. The words in verse 9 'But he said' are indicative of an ongoing strength; 'said' is in the perfect tense, which means that the experience is an ongoing comfort to his soul and the 'sufficient' word in that verse can also mean 'satisfied' – so that God is not promising just enough grace to get us through but a deeper balm to our soul that springs from knowing God is in this experience and we are in His will.

The whole of these verses are worth pondering deeply on our knees in worship. Here we see the overriding desire of Paul to know the power of Christ and to glorify Christ. That power and that glory are not in deliverance from suffering but in suffering itself. We should appreciate humbly that when we pray for power, this may be the way God intends us to receive it. If we only think of power in terms of deliverance we may miss the blessing and glory God has planned and intended in our lives.

Fruit is always the test

Before Paul lays down his pen and lets go of this counterblast to the false apostles he still has some things to say. The emphasis on signs rather than fruit, on 'miracle power' rather than 'endurance power' still concerns him.

He can produce evidence for both sides of the discussion. Signs, wonders and miracles had been done among them by Paul and these were apostolic signs (the signs and miracles in the New Testament only being done by the apostles or apostolic delegates). The trouble was that they had become so caught up with that sort of evidence that they seemed to have lost sight of basic Christian fellowship – the fruit of the Spirit – and Paul fears (verse 20) that there may be quarrelling, jealousy, outbursts of anger, factions, slander, gossip, arrogance and disorder amongst them. He then adds his fears of finding those earlier condemned for impurity, sexual sin and debauchery still around in the church and still not having repented of their sin.

Super-spiritual experience diverts from real living in obedience to Christ. I was pestered at one house-party years ago by a caretaker who regarded himself as far superior spiritually to all the rest of us. He was a pain in the neck as he pressed his apparently exuberant experience on us – but before the houseparty ended he was caught thieving and later was shown to be an adulterer. Corinth had a few like that too. Fruit is always the test and so Paul will be looking for this and teaching on it and disciplining over it when he comes to them in person. This will be in the love and concern of a father to his children (v. 14), but that will not weaken his reproof of sin and his action against those who had gone on sinning in spite of his earlier warnings (13:1–2).

Notice Paul's care that a charge will have to be supported by the testimony of two or three witnesses, as Jesus commands in Matthew 18:16. This is a wise word of caution over discipline. If leaders react and form a judgement on the testimony of one person, or on a rumour, they may find themselves acting unjustly. It is often a painful and heart-troubling business when we have to deal with matters of moral abuse or theft or something of that kind, but to ignore it is to encourage its repetition. Should anybody in Corinth hope that Paul in his physical weakness would also show weakness in his dealing with them they will be mistaken.

Paul spells out the weakness-power combination in a slightly different way in 13:3–4. Christ was crucified in weakness but he is now the Lord of power and authority. Similarly, we are weak in Christ and at the same time strong in Christ to serve him and the church. Power is again linked to the inner and spiritual rather than to the outward and physical.

Time for examination

There has been a lot of straight speaking from Paul. It demands a response. Paul is not able to be there at the moment the letter is read even though he hopes to go to Corinth before long. So he puts the onus of response on his hearers. They are to examine themselves (13 v. 5) – not in morbid introspection but rather as a sober self-examination of how they stand before Christ.

Introspection is an end in itself but self-examination is a means to an end. The basic test is that 'Christ is in us' – do we know that to be true or do we fail? If we know it to be true then we should see this to be true in others with whom we may not always see eye to eye – and Paul hopes they will acknowledge that Christ is in him too! The Corinthians might consider Paul a failure (they did, amazing though that seems to us, but it shows what 'spiritual superiority' can do to our powers of judgement!). Paul gently says that even if they think that, it is no excuse for them not to desire to live as the Lord intends. His prayer (v. 9) is for their perfection or 'improvement' (RSV). It is a penetrating phrase. Whatever they may think, he knows they have a long way to go and he prays that they may go forward and not stay in their present self-satisfied state. When he comes to them (v. 10) he will aim to build them up, for maturity in Christ is a heart desire of Paul for every Christian.

And so – farewell

His final greeting also tells them to aim at perfection or completeness. The loss of that ambition in a Christian can only result in a stultified Christian faith. It is always a great joy to meet older Christians who have not lost their hunger to know more of God and to grow in likeness to Christ and usefulness for him. Again, Paul urges them to listen to his appeal – he knows what he is up against. In his other appeals, the expressions of love and peace, the urging to greet one another with a holy kiss (or a good handshake all round or a great hug) he longs for them to be in the openness of peace and love that should mark the life of a church family anywhere.

The Grace

The last verse is known to us as 'The Grace'. It is a frequent habit in Christian circles to 'say the grace together' and in the church fellowship I belonged to at All Souls we used to grip one another's hands around the vast gathering when we said it at the end of a prayer gathering. Perhaps we say it so often that we do not ponder what we are praying for one another. 'The grace of our Lord Jesus Christ' reminds us particularly of that sentence we read in chapter 8 'you know the grace of our Lord Jesus Christ . . . though he was rich, he became poor.' We bathe in the glorious wonder of all that meant to us when we came to Christ and all it continues to mean to us as we enjoy the daily blessings of being in Christ and knowing his self-giving love towards us. The 'love of God' is a phrase whose depths will never be plumbed for eternity – richly enfolding us in all that His love means, He assures us afresh that nothing in all creation can separate us from that love. The 'fellowship of the Holy Spirit' is again one of the constant privileges of being in Christ – that we can know a bond that stretches across time and space, that unites us to millions we have never met and which enables us to see barriers broken down in the local fellowship of believers. The whole wonderful expression embraces the totality of life in Christ as part of the family of God and so how better can I end than saying it to you: May the grace of the Lord Jesus Christ, and the love of God, and the fellowship of the Holy Spirit be with you all.

LOVING GOD

Charles Colson

Loving God is the very purpose of the believer's life, the vocation for which he is made. However loving God is not easy and most people have given little real thought to what the greatest commandment really means.

Many books have been written on the individual subjects of repentence, Bible study, prayer, outreach, evangelism, holiness and other elements of the Christian life. In **Loving God**, Charles Colson draws all these elements together to look at the entire process of growing up as a Christian.

Combining vivid illustrations with straightforward exposition he shows how to live out the Christian faith in our daily lives. **Loving God** provides a real challenge to deeper commitment and points the way towards greater maturity.

THROUGH DAVID'S PSALMS

Derek Prince

Derek Prince, internationally known Bible teacher and scholar, draws on his understanding of the Hebrew language and culture, and a comprehensive knowledge of Scripture, to present 101 meditations from the Psalms.

Each of these practical and enriching meditations is based on a specific passage and concludes with a faith response. They can be used either for personal meditation or for family devotions. They are intended for all those who want their lives enriched or who seek comfort and encouragement from the Scriptures.

If you wish to receive *regular information* about *newbooks*, please send your name and address to:

London Bible Warehouse
PO Box 123
Baskingstoke
Hants RG23 7NL

Name _____

Address _____

_____

_____

_____

I am especially interested in:
- [ ] Biographies
- [ ] Fiction
- [ ] Christian living
- [ ] Issue related books
- [ ] Academic books
- [ ] Bible study aids
- [ ] Children's books
- [ ] Music
- [ ] Other subjects

P.S. If you have ideas for new Christian Books or of products, please write to us too!